THE SIXTH TRUMPETER

The Story
of Jezreel and his Tower

Also by P. G. Rogers

BATTLE IN BOSSENDEN WOOD: THE STRANGE STORY OF
SIR WILLIAM COURTENAY

The Sixth Trumpeter

THE STORY OF JEZREEL
AND HIS TOWER

P. G. ROGERS

London
OXFORD UNIVERSITY PRESS
NEW YORK   TORONTO
1963

Oxford University Press, Amen House, London E.C.4

GLASGOW NEW YORK TORONTO MELBOURNE WELLINGTON
BOMBAY CALCUTTA MADRAS KARACHI LAHORE DACCA
CAPE TOWN SALISBURY NAIROBI IBADAN ACCRA
KUALA LUMPUR HONG KONG

© Oxford University Press 1963

PRINTED IN GREAT BRITAIN

'Yea, strange things and spectral may men have beheld in Jezreel!'

THOMAS HARDY

PREFACE

For just over three-quarters of a century, until it was demolished in 1961, the massive brick-built structure adorned with strange symbols which was known as 'Jezreel's Tower' stood near the top of Chatham Hill, exciting the curiosity of all who saw it.

My own acquaintance with this remarkable building began shortly after the First World War, when my parents moved into a house in the upper part of Gillingham which stood almost under the shadow of the tower. The building was then, as it had been for many years, in a state of ruin, and was an irresistible attraction to adventurous young boys, despite the usual notices which warned that trespassers would be prosecuted.

A small gang of us found it easy to wriggle our way through the paling-fence which surrounded the tower – and when we crossed the narrow strip of rough grassland which surrounded it, what thrills awaited us! First, we gazed uncomprehendingly at the crossed swords, the trumpets and scrolls and other curious symbols which were carved in stone on the lofty walls. When, daringly, we stepped through one of the gaping doors or windows into the interior, we were for a little while overawed and scared. Inside, the tower was a vast, square brickwork shell, over which a menacing silence seemed to brood, except when this was suddenly and harshly shattered by the noise of a pigeon leaving its nesting-place aloft in one of the innumerable holes left by dislodged bricks.

The strangeness of the building, and the uncanny silence, accentuated by the sudden reverberations of sound, would probably have put us off the place for ever, had we not found in the huge basement powerful incitements to adventure. Chief of these were a number of low brick-lined tunnels which had been constructed to serve as ventilating shafts. We used to crawl along

vii

these, holding guttering candles in our hands to lighten the gloom; and when we had reached a comfortable spot, used to sit down and have an illicit smoke – cigarettes, if we had been able to afford them; if not, 'smoking-cane' (the dried stems of the wild clematis, which used to make us cough and retch like wheezy old men).

When smoking palled there were other excitements to be had. The thick concrete floor above the basement had been demolished over a wide area, and only the great steel girders, about a foot wide, were left straddling the interior. Below them, about twelve feet underneath, a jumbled mass of broken masonry and rubble lay on the basement floor. The temptation to show off one's prowess by walking along the girders could not be withstood; and soon this foolhardy exploit became a regular 'dare' during the visits which the other boys and I paid to the tower.

Then, one day, the inevitable happened. One of the gang fell from a girder on to the jagged lumps of stone below. His life was saved; but to this day he carries in his head a silver plate as a memento of his fall. After that disastrous escapade, of course, further visits to the tower were strictly forbidden; but I never lost my interest in the building and the people – James Jershom Jezreel, Queen Esther, and Prince Michael – who had been chiefly connected with it.

My adolescent curiosity found plenty of tales to sustain it, for the most absurd and unfounded rumours circulated in the Medway Towns about the Jezreelites and their tower. When I grew older I looked for a full and objective account of the sect, but found that there was none. In the late 1930s I began, therefore, to collect material for a book on the subject, but the outbreak of the Second World War put a stop to my researches and I had to lay my notes aside. Then, after many years had passed, I read in 1960, to my sorrow, that the tower was being demolished. Fired by this regrettable news I resumed my researches: and the result is the present book.

I would like to take this opportunity to express my thanks for the help I have received. A number of local inhabitants answered an appeal which I made in the Press, and sent me their interesting recollections of the sect and the tower. I thank my correspondents for their kind co-operation; and hope they will understand that, for reasons of space, I cannot mention each one of them by name.

I am very grateful also to Mr. Newnes the Town Clerk, and Mr. Mellilieu the Borough Treasurer of Gillingham, Mr. Shutt, the Secretary of the Gillingham Co-operative Society, and Colonel Sandeman of the R.E. Corps Library, Chatham, for kindly answering various points which I raised with them. I am under a special debt of gratitude to Mr. Tomlinson, the Borough Librarian, and Mrs. Evans, in charge of the Reference Library, for the great trouble they took to answer my queries and to put important material at my disposal. In the United States, Mr. Babcock, who has charge of the Burton Historical Collection in the Detroit Public Library, very kindly gave me information about the American sources relating to the sect. For the illustration depicting the tower as it looked when further work on it was stopped I am indebted to Mr. Shutt; for permission to reproduce the other illustrations, to the Trustees of the British Museum.

In conclusion, to prevent any possible misunderstandings, I would like to make two explanatory statements. First, I am in no way related to the Rogers family who played such a prominent part in the history of the Jezreelite sect, and who, therefore, are frequently mentioned in the following pages. Secondly, the quotation from Thomas Hardy which is printed at the front of the book refers not to the *man* Jezreel but to the valley of the same name in northern Palestine. The quotation is taken from a poem entitled 'Jezreel' which Hardy wrote, and *The Times* published on September 27, 1918, to commemorate the conquest of the Valley of Jezreel by Allenby's cavalry during the last stages of the Palestinian campaign. The words of the poet are however so apposite to the man who called himself Jezreel, and who is one of the chief characters in my book, that I could not resist quoting them.

PHILIP ROGERS

4 February 1962

ix

CONTENTS

ILLUSTRATIONS

I

PRECURSORS OF A PROPHET

IN an age when the Bible is less widely and less frequently read than formerly, the passionate preoccupation of our forefathers with its visions, prophecies and enigmas seems, to many people, an antique foible both strange and sterile. Yet, particularly from the sixteenth century onwards, as a result of the Reformation and the spread of the printed book, many keen, curious and eccentric intellects devotedly applied themselves to the problems which the Bible poses.

Some of the most fascinating and baffling of these are to be found in Revelation: and among them two deserve special mention. Chapter XX of Revelation tells of the coming of the millennium, and the first resurrection, when an angel shall bind Satan in chains, and the martyrs shall live and reign with Christ for one thousand years, after which Satan shall be loosed again 'for a little season'. Chapter VII of Revelation, also, contains a prophecy which holds out hopes of a blissful future existence for a favoured few whom God has chosen. From each of the twelve tribes of Israel 12,000 are to be sealed, making 144,000 in all; and these are destined to serve God day and night, and never more to hunger or thirst.

In the mid seventeenth century speculation about the millennium and the gathering of the 144,000 were an important part of the doctrines of the 'Fifth Monarchy Men', one of the most curious of the many strange sects which flourished at the time of the Civil War and the Commonwealth. The Fifth Monarchy Men believed that four monarchies had already flourished and passed away – the Assyrian, the Persian, the Greek and the Roman – and that the Fifth Monarchy – the rule of the saints – was about to begin. During this period Christ would reign with the elect for the preordained period of one thousand years.

Because they fanatically believed that Cromwell's rule was only a brief prelude to the millennium, the Fifth Monarchy Men supported him at first. They became disillusioned however when he showed no inclination to allow the rule of the saints to begin; and they railed at him as only intemperate fanatics would have dared to do. In December 1653, for example, Christopher Feake, a leading Fifth Monarchy Man, spoke of Cromwell as 'the most dissembling and perjured villain in the world'. Another, John Rogers, when brought before Cromwell for opposing the Lord Protector, told him to his face to remember that he, too, would be judged, 'for the day of the Lord was near!'.

On the whole Cromwell showed remarkable tolerance towards these fanatics, even when their excesses developed from words into deeds. In 1651 one John Robins had tried to foster a mad scheme for leading the 144,000 sealed of the dispersed tribes of Israel back to the Holy Land. Though he proclaimed that the chosen were to train for their arduous journey on a diet of dry bread, raw vegetables and water, such was the temper of the times that many persons flocked to join him. Since public disorder threatened to break out, Robins and his wife (who firmly believed she was about to give birth to a messiah) and his leading followers were put in the house of correction at Clerkenwell to cool their ardour.

The same delusion about the return of the Jews to the Holy Land dominated Thomas Tany, a London goldsmith, who claimed that in November 1649 it had been divinely revealed to him that he was a Jew belonging to the tribe of Reuben. In April 1650 he enlarged on this by announcing that he had received a commission from God to lead the dispersed Jews back to the Holy Land, and to rebuild the temple in Jerusalem. In furtherance of these schemes he declared himself to be a High Priest, and to lend colour to this assumption of authority he even went to the length of circumcising himself. After a time he moved to Eltham, where in preparation for the return to the Holy Land, he erected tents for his followers, each tent being decorated with a symbol of one of the twelve tribes of Israel.

His extravagances did not end there, however. They culminated in an insane attack on the Houses of Parliament in December 1654, when, flourishing a rusty sword, Tany wounded a doorkeeper and several other people before he was put under restraint. This excess of zeal strained even Cromwell's capacity for toleration, and Tany was put in prison, where he was kept for several months. After his release, as sure of his mission as ever, he set sail for Holland to collect members of the lost tribes of Israel sojourning there, but he was drowned during the passage.

The most ambitious project of the Fifth Monarchy Men was undertaken in January 1661, when, under one of their leaders named Venner, about fifty of them tried to overthrow the government of the newly-restored Charles II, and set up at last the long-awaited Fifth Monarchy. The reaction of the authorities this time was swift and severe. Venner himself was hanged and quartered before the meeting-house where he had been wont to preach. Ten of his followers were executed at the same time; and this demonstration of governmental ruthlessness so intimidated the remaining members of the sect that it began to decline, and finally broke up altogether.

The doctrines which had formed the basis of the Fifth Monarchy Men's activities merely went into abeyance, however. It needed only another period of uncertainty and violence to bring them out again into the light of day, this time elaborated and refurbished by visionaries of a different and later age. The new period of uncertainty and violence was inaugurated by the outbreak of the French Revolution at the end of the eighteenth century; and the Revolutionary and Napoleonic Wars which followed kept Europe in a state of turmoil for many years. The conditions were ideal for nurturing visionaries who discerned in the contemporary conflicts the 'voices, and thunders, and lightnings' referred to in Revelation xvi, 18. The 'voices' were not slow to make themselves heard; nor did they lack attentive listeners when they spoke, for the times were conducive to both strange conceits and contagious credulity.

3

One of the most interesting and engaging of the new generation of prophets was Richard Brothers. Born in Newfoundland
in 1757, he entered the Royal Navy when he was fourteen, and
served till 1783, when he was discharged on half-pay. He came to
London, lived quietly on his half-pay for a few years, and wor-
shipped regularly at a Baptist Chapel. Gradually however signs
of eccentricity appeared. He stopped drawing his pay, because he
objected to a sworn declaration which had to be made before-
hand. Next he cut by divine command a 'prophetic rod' from a
wild-rose tree; and forthwith he began to send prophecies to the
King, Queen, and Government. In 1793 his pretensions advanced
a further stage. He laid claim to descent from the family of Jesus
Christ, and because of this began to describe himself as 'God
Almighty's Nephew'. By 1794 however he had become engrossed
in the problem which exercised his mind and imagination for
many years. This was the fate of the lost tribes of Israel, dispersed among the nations after the collapse of the northern and
southern kingdoms of the Jews in ancient times.

Even when placed in a lunatic asylum in 1795 Brothers continued to pour forth his prophecies, to the effect that the dispersed Jews were to be found among the Gentile nations of
Europe, and that he, Brothers, was shortly to be revealed as
'Prince of the Hebrews' and would lead the Jews back to Palestine, and supervise the rebuilding of the temple in Jerusalem.
Brothers remained in the asylum till 1806, when he was released
owing to the good offices of friends. He devoted his remaining
years (he died in 1824) to abstruse and fantastic astronomical
calculations designed to elucidate biblical prophecies; but he
never quite forgot his earlier enthusiasm for 'ingathering' the
dispersed tribes of Israel. He is certainly one of the founders
of the 'British-Israelite' faith which flourished in different
forms throughout the nineteenth century, and is still alive
today.

More important than Brothers, however, in the line of progeni-
tors, was Joanna Southcott. Born in 1750, the daughter of a
Devonshire farmer, Joanna worked for a time as a shopgirl, and

4

then as a domestic servant. She had always been devout, and a regular churchgoer, but in 1792 her religious fervour took her into strange paths, and she began to turn out prophecies written in doggerel verse. Many of these she sealed, using a seal which she had picked up when she had been sweeping out a shop. The seal bore the initials I C (whence the fanciful might deduce Jesus Christ), with a star above and another below them.

Some of Joanna's prophecies were fulfilled; and this startling demonstration of her powers, and her own self-assurance, soon gained her many adherents, including men of good position, even clergymen of the Church of England. Fortified by their support, she settled in London, and in May 1802 began to seal the 144,000 who were to enjoy the millennial reign with Christ. The beginning of this, Joanna declared, was very near, and so, naturally enough, there were many applicants to be among the sealed. By 1808 Joanna had sealed several thousand persons, but then a misfortune occurred. One Mary Bateman who had been sealed was arrested on a charge of murder, was found guilty, and later hanged at York. This violent and dishonourable end of one of the sealed discredited the whole business, and the prophetess quickly stopped it.

She proceeded however to make use of an even more sensational means of self-advertisement. Already in 1802 she had vaguely asserted that one day she would bring into the world a spiritual man, the second Christ; but in 1813, in her *Third Book of Wonders*, she specifically stated that she was soon to give birth to Shiloh. This was a reference to Genesis xlix, where Jacob, on his deathbed, addresses his sons and says (verse 10): 'The sceptre shall not depart from Judah, nor a lawgiver from between his feet, until Shiloh come; and unto him shall the gathering of the people be.' The manner of Shiloh's birth was, according to Joanna, forecast in Revelation xii, 1–2:

'And there appeared a great wonder in Heaven; a woman clothed with the sun, and the moon under her feet, and upon her head a crown of twelve stars. And she being with child cried, travailing in birth, and pained to be delivered . . .

In October 1813, in preparation for her travail, Joanna went into seclusion, attended only by members of her own sex. Gradually excitement mounted, not only among her followers, but also among the public at large. In August 1814 matters had reached a stage when no fewer than nine doctors were called in to pronounce on Joanna's condition. A sensation was caused when six of the doctors gave it as their considered opinion that Joanna was displaying symptoms which in a younger woman would undoubtedly be proof of pregnancy. Joanna was sixty-four, so the caution of the six doctors was perhaps justified. But to Joanna's devoted followers the pronouncement meant only one thing: the biblical prophecies, as Joanna had foretold, were about to be fulfilled. With tremendous enthusiasm funds were collected to ensure that the birth of Shiloh should take place in the style which the circumstances demanded. Over £200 was spent on a magnificent cradle for the infant, and a costly Bible, specially produced, was also held ready for him.

Fiasco, however, and not fruition was approaching for Joanna; and on November 19, 1814 she had a premonition of death. She instructed her followers, if she should die, to keep her body warm for four days to make sure that death had really taken place. If so, she then directed, doctors were to make an examination of her body to find out why Shiloh had not appeared. Joanna's premonition turned out to be correct, for she died on December 27. The body was kept warm by means of hot-water bottles for the prescribed period, and then a post-mortem examination was carried out. To the amazement and consternation of her followers, not the slightest sign of pregnancy was revealed!

This difficulty was soon resolved by the faithful, for they claimed that Shiloh had really been born, but had been taken up to heaven at once. He would, in due course, reappear on earth to carry out his mission of redemption. Soon, as can be readily imagined, would-be Shilohs appeared and demanded recognition from the Southcottians. Soon, too, would-be prophets arose who claimed to be successors of Joanna and interpreters of her word.

6

Two of the many pretenders, George Turner and William Shaw, who flourished in the decade following Joanna's death, were accorded a measure of recognition by Joanna's followers, and these two men were accepted as authentic prophets.

The pseudo-Shilohs fared not so well. Though they glibly asserted that in accordance with Revelation xii, 5 Shiloh had been 'caught up unto God' to save him from the dragon which was ready to devour him at birth, they failed to convince the Southcottians that the divine offspring had materialized in their persons to carry out the work of redemption of the 144,000. There was however one exception. John Ward, a shoemaker, proclaimed himself Shiloh in 1827, and attracted a few followers. He soon adopted the style of 'Zion Ward', but despite the title, and his far-reaching claims, he still had few followers when he died in 1837.

Much more important from the point of view of the subsequent development of 'Christian-Israelite' doctrines was John Wroe, who was born in Yorkshire in 1782. He was the son of a small farmer, and as a young man became attracted to Southcottian doctrines. He regularly attended meetings of the sect in Yorkshire, and when Turner died in 1821, Wroe had impressed himself on his fellow-members to such an extent that some of them accepted him as successor to Turner as 'prophet' and interpreter of the Southcottian faith. Wroe soon attracted a strong following at Ashton-under-Lyne, and he built this up with all the skill of a born showman. He let his hair and beard grow long, to give himself the appearance of a biblical prophet; and in 1824, following the precedent of Thomas Tany, he was circumcised in the presence of his followers at Ashton. From then on Wroe insisted that all who followed him should also let their hair and beards grow long, undergo circumcision, and obey the Mosaic Law without exception. In other ways too Wroe elaborated on the 'Christian-Israelite' theme. He divided his followers into twelve tribes, and he built a sanctuary or temple, which cost £10,000, at Ashton. His followers had to wear a special dress, and Wroe devised a special ceremonial which had to be followed in

7

the sanctuary and other places where his teachings were practised. Gradually Wroe built up a large following, known as the
'Christian-Israelites', and though most of his supporters were in
the north of England, flourishing groups were soon started
among Southcottians in the south of England too. Kent in particular nourished a number of small Wroeite communities, in
particular at Chatham, Maidstone and Gravesend.

In 1830 Wroe had to leave Ashton because of an unsavoury
scandal involving three young girls in his flock. Many of the
Christian-Israelites continued to accept him as a divinely-inspired
prophet, however, and he merely transferred his headquarters
from Ashton to Wrenthorpe, near Wakefield. From here he
made, during the remaining years of his life, many long missionary journeys both at home and abroad. As a result he made still
more converts, especially in the United States and Australia. It
was in the latter country, in 1863, that Wroe died.

The widely-scattered sheep were now without their shepherd,
and circumstances were clearly very favourable for anybody with
the requisite personality and push to step in as successor. It is
not surprising therefore that a claimant eventually appeared. The
story of how he emerged from obscurity and established his claim
is of no little interest, because of the mystery which surrounded
him then, and has never since been satisfactorily cleared up.

II

THE FLYING ROLL

I N a memorable passage in *Pickwick Papers*, Mr. Pickwick, giving his impressions of the Medway Towns, observes:

'The principal productions of these towns appear to be soldiers, sailors, Jews, chalk, shrimps, officers and dockyard men. The commodities chiefly exposed for sale in the public streets are marine stores, hard-bake, apples, flat-fish, and oysters. The streets present a lively and animated appearance, occasioned chiefly by the conviviality of the military. It is truly delightful to a philanthropic mind to see these gallant men staggering along under the influence of an overflow both of animal and ardent spirits. . . .'

Mr. Pickwick, true to his benevolent nature, forbore to enlarge on the subject. It is not surprising, perhaps, for the overflow of animal and ardent spirits among the 'brutal and insolent soldiery' had an ugly aspect, which gained for Chatham an unenviable notoriety throughout the latter part of the nineteenth century. Drunkenness was widespread, and led to frequent affrays, some serious, in which soldiers, sailors and marines fought one another, or turned impartially on civilians. The sight of the naval or military patrol, frogmarching delinquents to barracks or police cell, was so common that it hardly aroused comment among passers-by. Amidst all these scenes of violence Venus, in the person of numerous prostitutes, danced attendance on Mars; and the repercussions of this evil in the town even reached Westminster, for questions were asked in the House about certain licensed premises which, it was alleged, were functioning also as brothels.

By 1876 the second battalion of the 16th Foot (the Bedford-shire Regiment) had been stationed in Chatham for such a long

9

time that it might well be thought that the men had become demoralized by the place. Nevertheless, to quote the cautious comment of the *Chatham and Rochester Observer* of February 5, 1876, they had 'upon the whole maintained a fair character'. This comment had been occasioned by the news that on February 3 the battalion was to leave Chatham, at last, for India. In accordance with the custom then prevailing, the men were given their arrears of pay a day or two before the battalion's departure. The result of this generous but unwise gesture by the army pay authorities was inevitable. On Monday afternoon, January 31, the men were paid; on Monday evening, the *Chatham and Rochester Observer* reported (February 5):

'Many conducted themselves in a most riotous manner in the town. At a quarter past nine there were fifty-four reported absent without leave, two of the number were taken into custody by the police, and were brought before the magistrate on the following morning. Another under the influence of drink mounted a cart which happened to be standing in the street, and drove off, but had not proceeded far before he fell out . . .'

The next morning there were no fewer than sixty prisoners in the guardroom, and it took some time before all these were suitably dealt with. Finally, however, on the duly appointed date, Thursday, February 3, the battalion marched to Chatham Station to entrain. They were preceded by the band of the Royal Engineers, which, with a fine sense of the occasion, struck up a rousing tune entitled 'You'll remember me!' . . . Another band, that of the third battalion of the 6oth Rifles, followed the warriors on to the departure platform of Chatham Station, and as the troop-train pulled out, rendered 'Auld Lang Syne', while the Bedfordshires waved and whistled and shouted till their train disappeared into the tunnel farther down the line.

Amongst the departing rank and file of the battalion was James Rowland White, who had only very recently enlisted. He was very reticent to his comrades about his antecedents, and he maintained this reticence, so that very little can be said with certainty about his early life. It seems most likely that he was born in 1840; and he was the son of a warehouse superintendent, so he later declared on his marriage certificate. Where he was born, whether he had brothers and sisters, and where he received his education, he never disclosed. According to one account which he is said to have given in later life, he was left an orphan at an early age, and taken care of by a family named White, from whom he took his own name. He was also reported to have said, on another occasion, that he had held a good position in a bank in the United States, but had felt impelled to come to England. He had worked his passage as a ship's stoker, and on his arrival in England had been commanded in a vision to enlist in the army. There is perhaps some truth in this story, for from time to time White revealed traces of transatlantic influence, particularly in his spelling. Nevertheless White's origin and early years remain a mystery, and it is not until 1875, when he enlisted in the 16th Foot, and came to Chatham, that the uncertainties cease.

Private White, unlike many, perhaps most of his comrades, was of serious disposition and felt no inclination to spend his leisure hours in the beershop and brothel. In some way or another he came to hear of the existence in Chatham of a small South-cottian sect, which called itself the 'New House of Israel', the trustees or leaders of which were a Mr. and Mrs. Head. Chatham had been one of the first provincial towns to form a South-cottian group, and after the death of the prophetess the faithful continued to meet, and eventually became followers of John Wroe, whom they considered a divinely-inspired successor of Joanna. The scandal in which Wroe became involved in 1830, however, destroyed their faith in him, and the Chatham Group renamed itself the 'New House of Israel' to distinguish itself from the 'Old House' which continued to follow Wroe.

Mr. and Mrs. Head lived in a house on Chatham Hill; and on October 13, 1875, Private James White knocked on their door and (to quote Mrs. Head) 'seriously inquired the way to salva-tion'. He was asked inside, for opportunities of making converts rarely came Mr. and Mrs. Head's way, and the chance of adding an extra member to their little band of followers was not to be missed. The information which Private White was given pleased him so much that there and then he eagerly asked to be allowed to join the 'New House of Israel'. Keen though she was to make a convert, Mrs. Head acted circumspectly. She handed her visitor some literature to study, including a 'book of laws' which laid down all the rules which had to be followed by members, and told him to come back when he had read all this matter, and had come to a firm decision.

On October 15 Private White called again at the house on Chatham Hill, announced that he had duly read all the literature provided, understood it, and accepted both the tenets of the faith and the rules of the sect. Immensely gratified, Mrs. Head forthwith enrolled him into the 'New House of Israel', little knowing what a cuckoo she had thereby introduced into the nest! Perhaps if she had been quicker-witted she might have felt some premonition of unease when, as Private White signed his name in the roll of members, he declared with great earnestness to Mrs. Head:

'Keep nothing from me, for I mean to make a speedy work!'

The implications of this enigmatic statement were however soon to be revealed. The 'New House of Israel' met regularly at the house of a relative of Mrs. Head in New Brompton, or Gillingham as it is now called, and the new convert attended with flattering regularity and diligence. On Christmas Eve, after one of the meetings, one of the members called Mrs. Head into another room, and there broke to the unsuspecting trustee the shattering news that Private White had set himself up as the 'Messenger of the Lord', and had requested all the members of the group to assemble on the morning of Christmas Day to hear him read extracts from his *Flying Roll*.

Mr. and Mrs. Head were scandalized by what they regarded as White's effrontery; and making use of their authority as trustees they immediately expelled him from the 'New House of Israel'. The consequences of this angry act were however disastrous for them. Since joining the little group of believers Private White had used his time and his persuasive powers to such good effect that all the members, including Mrs. Head's own relatives, numbering eighteen in all, followed him into the new path; and the two luckless trustees were left standing alone.

Among Private White's followers were two sisters, Clarissa Esther Rogers, aged fifteen, and her younger sister Elizabeth, aged thirteen. They were the daughters of Edward Rogers, a sawyer in Chatham Dockyard, and Elizabeth Ann, his wife. These were both members of the 'New House of Israel', and lived in humble circumstances in one of Baker's Cottages near the Ash Tree public house, not far from the top of Chatham Hill. The relatives of Mrs. Head who lived in Gillingham were friendly with the Rogers family, and they grew so fond of little Clarissa that they finally persuaded her parents to allow her to come and live with them in Gillingham. Here the girl attended the meetings of the 'New House of Israel', and immediately fell under the sway of the tall, well-built private from the 16th Foot. Clarissa and her younger sister went for long walks with White, and listened entranced whilst he discoursed fluently on the Bible, his own message, and the future.

At this time, after he had disclosed that he was the 'Messenger of the Lord', White adopted the style of 'James Jershom Jezreel' for the purpose of the religious activities in which he indulged outside the barrack gate. The choice of these names was as curious as it was revealing. 'James' may well have been his own name; but 'Jershom' he took from Exodus xviii, 2–3:

'Then Jethro, Moses' father-in-law, took Zipporah, Moses' wife, after he had sent her back,
'And her two sons; of which the name of the one was Gershom; for he said, I have been an alien in a strange land . . .'

The name was intended to signify that White, or Jezreel, was a 'stranger'; for, as he frequently explained, the most faithful and devout men from Abraham onwards were called, or called themselves, 'strangers', because they had been set apart by God to do his will. Strangers in this sense were, therefore, 'men after God's

13

own heart', and 'especially blessed'. White changed 'Gershom' to 'Jershom' because of the alliterative effect, but also because 'J' was an initial of special significance (Joanna Southcott, John Wroe). Also, it seems, the 'J' was decided upon because it enabled the 'Messenger' to sign his initials JJJ with a continuous line at the top, signifying the iron rod of the prophet.

The choice of the third name, 'Jezreel', was even more recondite than that of the second. It was derived from Hosea i, 2–5, 10–11:

'... And the Lord said to Hosea, Go, take unto thee a wife of whoredoms and children of whoredoms: for the land hath committed great whoredom, departing from the Lord.

'So he went and took Gomer the daughter of Diblaim; which conceived, and bare him a son. And the Lord said unto him, Call his name Jezreel; for yet a little while, and I will avenge the blood of Jezreel upon the house of Jehu, and will cause to cease the kingdom of the house of Israel.

'And it shall come to pass at that day that I will break the bow of Israel in the valley of Jezreel ...

'Yet the number of the children of Israel shall be as the sand of the sea, which cannot be measured or numbered; and it shall come to pass that in the place where it was said unto them, Ye are not my people, there it shall be said unto them, Ye are the sons of the living God.

'Then shall the children of Judah and the children of Israel be gathered together, and appoint themselves one head, and they shall come up out of the land; for great shall be the day of Jezreel ...'

One of Jezreel's favourite quotations came from Joel ii, 1:

'Blow ye the trumpet in Zion, and sound an alarm in my holy mountain: let all the inhabitants of the land tremble: for the day of the Lord cometh, for it is nigh at hand.'

Throughout his life he made great play with the symbolism of the trumpet – partly, no doubt, owing to his army experiences. He claimed to be the sixth trumpeter who had sounded the alarm, the others who had preceded him being Richard Brothers, Joanna Southcott, George Turner, William Shaw, and John Wroe.

The trumpet was blown, however, to draw attention to the message which the trumpeter had to bring: and in Jezreel's case this message was contained in a mysterious 'Flying Roll'. According to a statement made later to the Press by an ex-follower of White, the latter wrote the first part of the *Flying Roll* in the mundane surroundings of a house in Trafalgar Road, Gillingham. The blinds of the room in which he sat writing down his 'message' were drawn close; and for twelve days and nights, while he laboured in the throes of composition, nobody was allowed to enter the room or to have any contact with him at all. This self-immurement was carried to such lengths that his food was left outside the door, and when he had finished a meal he placed the empty dishes outside again to be taken away.

Before White could complete his *Flying Roll* he learned that his battalion was to be posted to India in February 1876. This was a grievous blow to his little group of followers, who now called themselves the 'New and Latter House of Israel'; but White consoled them by promising to maintain regular contact with them, and by promising, moreover, to transmit further instalments of the message contained in the *Flying Roll*.

This name he took partly from Jeremiah xxxvi, which relates how the Lord commanded the prophet Jeremiah to take a roll of a book and write in it all the words the Lord had spoken unto him. When the roll was read to King Jehoiakim of Judah the king was so displeased that he cast it into a fire. Thereupon the Lord commanded Jeremiah:

'Take thee again another roll, and write in it all the former words that were in the first roll, which Jehoiakim the King of Judah hath burned.'

The other source of inspiration for the name *Flying Roll* was Zechariah v, 1–2:

'Then I turned, and lifted up mine eyes, and looked, and behold a flying roll.

'And he (an angel) said unto me, What seest thou? And I answered,

15

I see a flying roll; the length thereof is twenty cubits, and the breadth thereof ten cubits.'

The message contained in the *Flying Roll* of Jezreel was directed to the scattered tribes of Israel. These consisted of the descendants or 'remnant' of the ten which had formed the ancient kingdom of Israel in the north of Palestine, but also of some of the descendants of the other two (Judah and Benjamin) which formed the southern kingdom of Judah, and from whom the Jews, as distinct from the 'Israelites' were descended. The favoured few, numbering 144,000 in all, would achieve true immortality – that is, redemption of body, soul and spirit, and would not suffer death.

Patriotically, the *Flying Roll* declared that that part of the 'remnant' in England would be saved first:

'Blow the Trumpet in this land of England first, and say "England! The day of thy judgement is come: thou shalt be the first to be judged and the first to be redeemed. England! Thou art the land of Joseph, the granary of the Lord's corn, wine, honey and milk. All Israel shall be driven into this land; there shall 144,000 bones of the Virgin be gathered, when the Trumpet of War shall sound over the earth, but no foreign sword shall enter thy borders!" '

(Flying Roll, Vol. I, Preface, xvi.)

The ten tribes of Israel had been scattered after the fall of the ancient northern kingdom, said Jezreel, and as a result of their wanderings during hundreds of years their descendants had completely lost sight of their origins and identity. God however had promised (Isaiah xi, 11) 'to recover the remnant of his people' at the appointed time. God had promised Jacob (Isaiah xliv, 3–5) that he would bless his offspring, of whom 'one shall say I am the Lord's; and another shall call himself by the name of Jacob; and another shall subscribe with his hand unto the Lord, and surname himself by the name of Israel'. This promise indicated, said Jezreel, that there were three churches: the first Christian, the second Jewish, and the third comprising the 'remnant' of the scattered ten northern tribes, and a few from the two southern. These members of the third church, now scattered among the

Gentiles, would receive special marks of God's favour denied to Christians and Jews. This advantage was due to the fact that members of the third church (the 'New and Latter House of Israel', of course) observed *both* the Mosaic Law and the Gospel, whereas the Jews rejected the Gospel, and the Christians did not accept the Law. The special favour, to be accorded to 12,000 from each of the twelve tribes, was full redemption. They would be sealed in their foreheads, and would form the immortal Bride of Christ, reigning with him for one thousand years. They were, in fact, the 144,000 bones, called Israel. (*Flying Roll*, Vol. III, p. 89.)

As for all others than the favoured 144,000, said Jezreel, their bodies would decay and disappear for ever after death, though they would enjoy a measure of salvation through their souls being reunited with their spirits, either at the first or the second resurrection. At the first resurrection the souls of the unrighteous would be cast back into the pit, and they would have to wait for the second resurrection, at the end of the millennial reign of Christ, for their limited measure of salvation. But all, Jezreel, promised, would eventually achieve this.

Jezreel did not hesitate to proclaim, dramatically, that the time of the 'ingathering' of the 144,000 was nigh.

'We proclaim to all the nations of the earth that the time is now come (the third watch) that the people of God shall no longer perish, but that the time has arrived when the last enemy death shall be destroyed . . .' (*Flying Roll*, Vol. I, p. 24.)

'The people of God are called upon through this message of "The Flying Roll" to stand for their lives . . . and they will stand, and not perish.' (*Flying Roll*, Vol. I, p. 84.)

The reference to the 'third watch' came from Luke xii, 37–38:

'Blessed are those servants whom the Lord when he cometh shall find watching. . . .
'And if he shall come in the second watch, or come in the third watch, and find them so, blessed are those servants.'

Jezreel calculated that mankind was now in the third watch, as

17

follows. First, the scriptural day was equivalent to one thousand years, for it was written in 2 Peter iii, 8:

'But, beloved, be not ignorant of this one thing, that one day is with the Lord as a thousand years, and a thousand years as one day.'

God had created the earth in 4004 B.C. The six days of creation equalled six thousand years, and these had been divided into three dispensations. The first two had stretched from the fall of Adam to the death of Christ, a period of about four thousand years. Thus man was now living in the third and final dispensation. As was written in Hosea ix, 7:

'The days of visitation are come, the days of recompence are come; Israel shall know it . . .'

The scriptural day of one thousand years was divided into twelve hours, thus each hour was 83 years 4 months long. The hour, in turn, was divided into four quarters or watches, each of which was 20 years 10 months. The 10th hour had ended in April 1833, and the 11th had begun. The third watch of the 11th hour had begun in 1875, so that little time remained in which to carry out the work of 'ingathering' the 144,000 who were to be granted full redemption.

Jezreel's followers in England eagerly waited for and carefully preserved the various instalments of his 'message' as they arrived from India; and soon it was decided to publish them as *Extracts from the Flying Roll*, to be completed in twelve long sermons. Volume I contained the first sermon, which was divided into seven parts, designed to initiate the reader into the intricacies of the faith:

'A perfect knowledge of the deep mysteries of the Kingdom is not to be obtained by stopping at "first principles", neither can the city be measured by reading this first volume only. Like the parable in the Book of Ezekiel we must enter the "deep waters" gradually . . . the best wine being reserved till the last. It was absolutely expedient to compile the *Flying Roll* in its present form of "Extracts" otherwise it could never be understood. To obtain a perfect knowledge of the fourth volume which is *the* Flying Roll you must first study the three volumes of "Extracts" . . .' (Preface, p. xxviii.)

In an introduction to Volume I of the *Extracts* Mr. John E. Mouland wrote:

'I have caused it (Volume I) to be published because I have been commanded to do so, and bow in meekness and obedience to that authority. It is a source of great joy to me, that I, the least of all, have been so much blessed as to be a chosen instrument to hold in my possession the originals of *The Flying Roll*, and to be thus privileged, unworthy as I am, to offer them to the Gentile Churches in England, first: that the lost tribes of the House of Israel may hear the voice of their shepherd, gather themselves together, and flee to the city. The words of *The Flying Roll* are spirit and life . . . the children of Abraham will recognize the voice and rejoice . . . the words of this *Roll* which have been closed up and sealed till the time of the end, are now revealed to mankind, because the time for the fulfilment of "all things" is come . . .'

The author himself of the *Flying Roll* began Sermon One in Volume I by observing modestly:

'My dear hearers, before uttering any of those things which have been kept secret from the foundation of the world[1], we remind you that we do not set *"ourselves"* up above our fellows – nor do we wish to boast of any wisdom or knowledge, as coming from "ourselves"; none are more cognizant than we are of our utter unworthiness; still, it doth please the Lord . . .' (Vol. I, p. 2.)

In Part V of the first sermon Jezreel declared, using a homely metaphor:

'We propose to take the besom, and sweep away the thick layers of cobwebs which have been so long accumulating, and which have eclipsed the true light.' (Vol. I, p. 117.)

Shortly afterwards followed a proud forecast:

'Knowing that some of the strangers and seed of Israel are scattered

[1] A reference to Matthew xiii, 35: 'I will open my mouth in parables; I will utter things which have been kept secret from the foundations of the world.'

19

in every country on this planet – this Flying Roll will be translated into every tongue spoken by man. It has been ordered to be promulgated in England first, because the majority of the ten tribes have emigrated to the northern Isles . . .' (Vol. I, p. 121.)

The seventh and concluding part of the first sermon which constituted Volume I of *Extracts from the Flying Roll* ended with an impassioned appeal to the 144,000 of the dispersed tribes of Israel to rally to the 'Messenger':

'In these seven discourses or first sermon, we have only offered you the preface of that which is to come . . . these sermons will not be appreciated now by the Gentiles . . . but in a few days they will be sought for, and eagerly digested, while the House of Israel will be sought for – when the vials of the wrath of God will be poured out upon the earth, and all nations gathered together in battle. When the fiends of war will be let loose and the valley of Jehosophat will open wide her jaws and the blood of the slain and wounded will flow in the valleys; – for great and terrible will be the day of the Lord, which is now fast approaching. The world may cry out Peace! Peace! but there will be no peace, but war! war! with all its miseries, pestilences, famines and diseases; – nor will it be confined to Europe alone, but the whole planet will be one scene of bloodshed. . . . The eyes of the Gentiles will then be opened, when they shall see Israel on the Mount dwelling in peace and safety. . . . We exhort all the children of Abraham now in bondage under the Gentiles to "come out from among them" and be separate and to disengage themselves from the yoke of the Gentiles.' (Vol. I, pp. 200–202.)

Volume II of the *Extracts*, containing the second sermon, was introduced by Joseph Head, who addressed himself, grandly, to 'The English Public'.

'I would request all to note carefully,' he said, 'what is written in the *Flying Roll* concerning the earthquakes, famines, bloodshed, sorrows, troublous times, and the vials of God's wrath about to fall upon all the nations and kingdoms of the world. . . . We sound the trumpet, and call upon all the Spirits of the Just – the seed of Israel, the stock of Abraham – to flee for their lives to the city Jerusalem above. . . . Flee from the vials of God's wrath, which are about to be poured out in this third and last watch. . . .'

After all these rumblings of doom, Head's postscript came somewhat as an anti-climax:

'N.B. For the guidance of the outcasts of Israel and the dispersed of Judah – who seek to come up out of Egypt and join their "Brethren" and "their tribes". Information will be sent to anyone addressing themselves either by letter or personally, to the following head officers of the New and Latter House of Israel, namely:

Joseph Head	George Moore
John Rogers, Senior	Joshua Rogers

All letters must be prepaid.'

In his second sermon Jezreel repeated his warning that the third watch of the eleventh hour was soon due to end in frightful convulsions. England, however, would be spared the worst:

'All nations will soon be at war against each other, and dethrone their kings, and all nations will cry out "O happy England, England, what nation is like thee?" England will be the last country where there will be a king . . . then all nations will flock to England, and all Israel will be gathered *there;* and the vessels which they have prepared to carry men into many nations, will bring Israel home, home to the barn.' (Vol. II, p. 90.)

Joseph Head introduced Volume III of the *Extracts* to the public with the information that it contained 'still deeper and sublime teachings': and the author himself reinforced his message with the statement:

'So shall the words of the former Messenger of Israel (John Wroe) spoken on the 5th of the 7th month 1833 be fulfilled: "For the Flying Roll shall go through the land; it shall be swift and powerful. And he that signs not this Roll, his name is death: for this Roll is life, and it shall go from the north to the east, and from the west to the south.' (Vol. III, p. 96.)

The conclusion of Sermon Three, forming Volume III of the *Extracts,* was dated 'Ist of Ist Month 1881': and at this point publication of the remaining sermons was postponed, because Jezreel and his followers in England were busy preparing for his release from the army. At length the necessary formalities were concluded, and on November 4, 1881, Private James White, alias James Jershom Jezreel, said goodbye to the 16th Foot, and sailed from Calicut to England.

The parting was without regret on either side. During his service in India White had tried, in a spirit of remarkable optimism, to convert some of the old sweats among his comrades. His attempts failed dismally; and though the tough warriors of the Bedfordshires admired him for his 'cleverness', they had no liking for him. White was quite undismayed. He knew that he was returning to a faithful flock on whom he could utterly depend; and his mind was already busy with grandiose plans for the future.

III

GREAT SHALL BE THE DAY
OF JEZREEL

WHILE Private White had been away in India he had kept up a regular correspondence with Clarissa Rogers, one of his most ardent disciples. It must be assumed that during White's absence in India, if not indeed before he left Chatham with his regiment in February 1876, he and Clarissa had agreed to marry. If this assumption is not correct, the decision to marry must have been very sudden, for only a few weeks after he had returned to England, and had completed his discharge from the army, White married Clarissa Rogers.

The marriage took place in the Medway Register Office in Chatham, on December 17, 1881; and it is interesting to note that on the certificate White described himself as a bachelor, and gave his occupation as 'merchant's clerk'. He also gave his age wrongly, it would seem, as thirty-two. This was perhaps because he wished to conceal the considerable disparity between what was probably his real age, forty-one, and that of his bride, who was only twenty-one. On the marriage certificate, which was witnessed by Clarissa's father Edward, and a relative named Frances Rogers, the address of both bride and bridegroom was given as 2 Copenhagen Road, Gillingham; and here they both resided for a short time while they planned the grand campaign which was to bring converts and cash steadily trickling, if not flooding, into the 'New and Latter House of Israel'.

At first Jezreel (as White from now onwards invariably called himself) had thoughts of carrying on John Wroe's work in the former prophet's first headquarters, Ashton-under-Lyne. He appeared there one day shortly after his return to England, and handed the trustees of the 'Christian-Israelites' a copy of the

23

Flying Roll to read. To his amazement and anger, the trustees not only rejected it, but actually had the effrontery to burn it, as a sign of their disgust. Quoting Job xxxviii, 2, they compared Jezreel with Elihu, and asked:

'Who is this that darkeneth counsel by words without knowledge?'

To Jezreel's faithful followers the action of the Christian-Israelites at Ashton-under-Lyne was nothing short of sacrilege. As they declared afterwards, the Ashton brethren had 'rejected the message of the Lord, and cast out his Messenger'.

After the rebuff at Ashton Jezreel returned to Gillingham, which he now determined to make his headquarters. He badly needed converts to swell the numbers of his little band, and he boldly decided that a grand missionary tour in the United States would be the best means of getting them. This decision was not quite as startling and over-ambitious as it might appear to have been. In the spring of 1881 Clarissa Rogers, burning with her new faith, and restive because of the absence of the 'Messenger' in India, decided to visit the United States, a country where Wroe's 'Christian-Israelites' had obtained a footing, particularly in Michigan and other areas adjacent to the Great Lakes. There the zealous Clarissa hoped to win over adherents to the 'New and Latter House of Israel', both by preaching and by the distribution of copies of Volume I of *Extracts from the Flying Roll*.

She stayed with a Miss Easton in New York, and from this address copies of the *Flying Roll* were sent to various places in the United States, in the hope that they would be bought, read, and bring in converts. That hope was not disappointed. One morning in April 1881 Noah Drew, a Michigan farmer, noticed a copy of the *Flying Roll* on sale in the village store. For many years Drew had been a believer in John Wroe's doctrines, so he naturally bought Jezreel's book, and became an enthusiastic convert to its teaching. In fact he was so impressed by what he had read that he sent a letter to Miss Easton in New York asking for further information about the 'New and Latter House of Israel'. This was promptly supplied, and Noah Drew's conversion was complete. He, his wife and his sons became ardent believers, and Drew himself paid a visit to Miss Easton in New York. There he met Clarissa Rogers, 'the young English missionary' as Drew called her; and she made such a favourable impression on him that he invited her to accompany him back to his farm.

Clarissa was delighted to do so, and found the company of her host and his family so agreeable that she stayed three months with them. During this time she preached locally, she conducted services, and – Drew noted – spent much of her time writing letters to a person in India whom she described as 'The Stranger', or 'The Lord's Messenger'. At length Clarissa had to leave Drew and his family because, she said, the 'Stranger' or 'Messenger' was shortly returning from India to England, and she had to return to the latter country to meet him.

Clarissa came back to England much impressed with the possibilities of the United States as a field for missionary endeavours on behalf of the 'New and Latter House of Israel'. When therefore Jezreel's attempt to win acceptance at Ashton-under-Lyne was so uncompromisingly rejected, she tried to soothe his wounded pride by suggesting a tour in the United States. There, as she knew from experience, were simple folk who were much more pliable material to work on than the stiff-necked elders of Ashton.

Jezreel swiftly saw the possibilities, and so a letter was sent to Noah Drew in April 1882, asking if he would like to take part in an evangelistic tour with Mr. and Mrs. Jezreel. The farmer, hugely flattered, agreed; and as had been hoped, invited his two correspondents to make his farmhouse their headquarters. A few months later Jezreel and his wife arrived there, and preparations were at once made for the grand missionary tour.

Jezreel, with a fine feeling for the romantic, wanted everybody to travel on horseback. Drew, however, with a firmer grip on realities, managed to persuade the 'Messenger' to drop the idea, and to agree to covered wagons instead – less dashing, perhaps, but much more practical. Several wagons were bought, and were lengthened to provide more room for the impedimenta which

25

was to be carried. This comprised tents and many wooden benches, the cost of which, added to that of the wagons, amounted to a considerable sum. The enthusiastic Noah, and two of his sons (who between them contributed 700 dollars) bore most of this expense, and bore it cheerfully, for the good of the cause.

The day at length arrived when the little group of missionaries set off in their covered wagons, for all the world like a band of pioneers bound for the Wild West. The first stop was at a place called Howell, the capital of Livingston County, in the state of Michigan. The arrival of Barnum and Bailey's Circus could hardly have caused greater excitement; and the local inhabitants stood around and watched with tremendous interest as first one large tent was erected as stabling for the horses, and then a second, much larger, for the holding of the meetings. Because of this curiosity of the people, Jezreel had a packed audience for his first meeting, and was given a quiet and respectful hearing. But, the Press reported, few amongst his hearers seemed to grasp anything at all of what he was talking. . . .

Leaving this well-mannered but disappointingly unresponsive place the evangelists moved on to Brighton. Here they encountered hostility, and a mob assembled and threatened to cut the tents to pieces and assault the missionaries. Only Noah Drew's local knowledge, diplomatic attitude and conciliatory words to the crowd averted what was undoubtedly a very ugly situation; and even so some damage was done before the police managed to disperse the more disorderly elements. The police, fearing more trouble if the missionaries stayed, ordered them to leave Brighton immediately; so they struck their tents and departed for Detroit, some forty miles away to the north-west, in order to get well away from this hostile neighbourhood. By this time there was a certain amount of tension between Jezreel and Drew, so to avoid any exacerbation of this the 'Messenger' and his wife went on ahead by train, and waited in Detroit for Drew to arrive with the wagons.

At Detroit however further trouble developed over Noah Drew's youngest son. Jezreel (no doubt to flatter the father) had chosen the young lad to be his aide-de-camp; but Drew objected

26

strongly to Jezreel's edict that the boy should devote himself entirely to his duties, even if this meant that he saw little of his parents and friends. At length matters came to a head, there was a quarrel, and Jezreel and his wife packed all their belongings in a cab and departed from Detroit, leaving Noah Drew stranded with the wagon-train.

Drew went at once to Miss Easton in New York, to seek her counsel. He got cold comfort from that lady, however, so he returned to Detroit, where he arranged that for the time being the tents and other equipment should be stored in a warehouse. Noah Drew then returned with his wife to his farm, sad and stricken, but – incredibly – with his faith in the 'New and Latter House of Israel' undimmed.

As for Jezreel, he returned to England smarting bitterly from this second fiasco. 'The pearl of truth was offered to many,' he declared, 'but few received it. . . .' Nevertheless, inspired by the utter devotion of his wife and the small band of believers in Gillingham, Jezreel doggedly continued his proselytizing activities. He spent a good deal of his time in 1882 and 1883 visiting towns in England and Scotland, in an unwearied search for converts. But it was uphill work, and the converts entered the fold in disappointingly small numbers. Even so they came generally from established Southcottian groups, for Jezreel made little impression on the 'Gentiles'. In February 1883 Jezreel spent ten days in Lincoln, which was a stronghold of Wroe's Christian-Israelites, and he spoke on a number of occasions in the Co-operative Hall in the city. After all his efforts, however, only nineteen persons joined the 'New and Latter House of Israel' – and all these were Christian-Israelites. Since these comprised the majority of John Wroe's following in Lincoln, Jezreel must at least have had the satisfaction of knowing that the trustees in Ashton-under-Lyne would be much disturbed at this major secession.

In May 1883 Jezreel departed for Australia, a land where John Wroe had established a number of communities of Christian-Israelites. Assuming correctly that this previous indoctrination would render many of Wroe's followers susceptible to his own teachings, Jezreel laboured indefatigably in Australia, and had the satisfaction of winning over a good number of adherents to the 'New and Latter House of Israel'.

He soon returned to Gillingham, however, for he was determined to establish there as soon as possible a central headquarters which should attract the faithful from all parts of the world, and induce them to sell their possessions in order to come to Gillingham to live and work with the 'Messenger'. A first stage in the ambitious programme was reached on October 7, 1883, when a meeting-hall seating 200 people was opened at the junction of Nelson and Napier Roads in Gillingham. Private services were held here every Sunday evening for members of the 'New and Latter House of Israel', and in the afternoon for members of the public.

The 'open' services, as the latter were called, were very popular, partly because of the very good musical accompaniment provided. Jezreel was very fond of harp music; and violins and piccolos, as well as a harmonium, contributed to the effect. The public also attended the services from curiosity, however, especially as Jezreel had given great publicity to the importance which he attached to young children as teachers and preachers of his faith. This, he declared, was in accordance with Matthew xxi, 16:

'Out of the mouth of babes and sucklings thou hast perfected praise.'

The *Chatham and Rochester Observer* of May 17, 1884, reporting a service held on Sunday, May 11, said:

'The service in Israel's Hall, Napier Road, was largely attended on Sunday afternoon, when the proceedings were conducted by three little girls. Emma Petry, aged thirteen, of Stratford, took for her subject "The one widow, one leper, one hundred-fold, or 144,000 living bones". "The Mariner's Chart across the Trackless Ocean" was the subject on which Georgina Watson, aged twelve years, of Kilmarnock, Ayrshire, addressed the congregation; and Janet Watson, aged fourteen, also of Kilmarnock, spoke on "Why Christendom seeks Life through Death". The whole of the subjects were well treated, and were listened to with much pleasure. One of the most important features in the service was the excellence of the singing, which was led by a piano, six harps, four violins and a piccolo.'

As a result of Jezreel's untiring efforts to gain followers in Britain and abroad, the financial resources of the 'New and Latter House of Israel' began to swell. Accordingly, the 'Messenger' and his wife were able to move into 'Woodlands', a pleasant country house of moderate size standing in attractive grounds fronting on Woodlands Lane, Gillingham, which at that time was a real country lane, with open fields on either side.

Here, in this rural environment, Jezreel established 'Israel's International College', to which children of both sexes of members of the sect could be sent for education, or rather indoctrination. The 'college' was founded on March 1, 1884, and the number of pupils soon reached the respectable total of fifty, despite the fact that fees were £18 a quarter (though this included board and lodging). The education given by no means justified the grandiose title of the establishment. It was limited to a study of Jezreel's 'lately-revealed theological truths', musical training in the harp and other instruments, and lastly what Jezreel vaguely described as 'general practical knowledge'. The curriculum was thus as severely practical, if not as elaborate, as that of the medieval church schools; and as it was in the hands of Jezreel himself and only one schoolmaster, it was hardly likely to provide a liberal education. Nevertheless, Jezreel was inordinately proud of his 'college', and had a large board erected near the entrance drive of 'Woodlands', on which the name of the establishment was painted in large gilt letters on a black background. The boys and girls were dressed in a uniform of their own, and created a most favourable impression when they appeared in public because of their neat and clean appearance.

Jezreel had a genius for showmanship, and this was revealed, for example, when he decided to hold a series of open-air services during the summer months in the meadow in Woodlands Lane which lay opposite 'Woodlands'. He conceived the idea of erecting a pavilion in the meadow, to accommodate preachers, choir and orchestra; and he calculated, correctly as it turned out, that the many Gillingham citizens who normally took a Sunday stroll down Woodlands Lane would certainly halt awhile to listen to his service. The services were lavishly advertised. One notice which appeared in the *Chatham and Rochester Observer* on July 19, 1884, ran as follows:

GRAND INAUGURATION
for the
OPENING OF THE PAVILION
on the
27th July 1884, Sunday Evening at Six o'clock,
for
OPEN AIR PREACHING
IN THE MEADOW OPPOSITE TO
'THE WOODLANDS', GILLINGHAM, KENT.
The meeting will be opened (D.V.) by
GEORGINA WATSON
(Of Israel's International College, a little girl of 12 summers). Hymn, 'Strike the Harp' – Prayer – Opening Address. Subject – 'Foretaste of Dishes.'

HARRY FOX
(Of Israel's College, a boy of 13 summers.)
Subject – John xii.

JANET WATSON
(Of Israel's College, a girl of 14 summers.)
Hymn 21, page 66, 'Israel strike thy rusted lyre'. Subject – 'The Keys of the Kingdom.'

MRS. JEZREEL
will also address the meeting. Subject: 'A distinct and certain sound of the TRUMPET.' Hymn 17, 'All Hail the glorious frame'.

JAMES J. JEZREEL,
(Author of the *Flying Roll,* and Principal of Israel's International College) will next address the meeting. Subject: 'The Law and the Testimony.'

———————

The MUSIC will consist of Harpists, Piano, Piccolo, Violin, and Full Choir of Singers, conducted by Mrs. Jezreel. The meadow will be thrown open to the public at 6 p.m. Band playing. The preaching will commence at 6.30. The public are cordially invited. All seats free.

NO COLLECTION

Reserved seats can be obtained by Tickets issued FREE upon application at Beacon Court and Edina Villa, New Brompton, and at the 'Woodlands', Gillingham, and from members of the Society. Visitors are requested to enter by the gateway into the meadow by the road, not across the fields. Please go round by the Gillingham or Rainham Roads, then down the lane leading to the 'Woodlands'.

In an age which knew not the mixed blessings of cinema, radio and television, Jezreel's cleverly worded advertisement could hardly have failed to draw the crowds. Youthful prodigies, music, the great man and his wife themselves, – and definitely NO COLLECTION. There was no withstanding this powerful combination, and the open-air meeting was a huge success. The *Chatham and Rochester Observer* reporting it on Saturday, August 2, 1884, said:

'In the presence of a large concourse of spectators variously computed to number from 1,500 to 2,500 persons, the inauguration of a series of Sunday services in connection with a religious sect, the members of which style themselves the "New and Latter House of Israel" took place on Sunday evening last in the large meadow opposite the "Woodlands", Gillingham. A pavilion constructed of wood and canvas with annexes on either side was erected for the accommodation of those taking an active part in the proceedings. The main or centre erection contained the speakers and the instrumentalists, while in the annexes were seated the juvenile representatives of the new faith, some score or so of girls on the right hand, and a similar number of

31

boys on the left. The former were attired in dresses of a light brown colour, and wore straw hats with a scarlet band bearing the letters I.C. The boys' uniform consisted of a grey mixture with scarlet facings and gilt tassels, and hats similar to those worn by the girls.

Arranged in semicircular form in front of the pavilion were a number of cornsheaves, topped with fernleaves and flowers, the red-bordered and scalloped hangings of the roof of the buildings being festooned with figleaves. The general scene, taken in conjunction with the picturesque and sylvan surroundings, was one of an unusually effective character.

The evening's devotions were opened with a hymn, the instrumental accompaniment consisting of about a dozen harps with the addition of pianofortes, piccolo and violin, augmented by a choir of male and female adults. During the service, which lasted about two hours, addresses were delivered by Janet and Georgina Watson, aged respectively fourteen and thirteen (*sic*) years; Harry Fox, a boy of thirteen summers, and Mr. and Mrs. Jezreel. The extempore orations of the two damsels, in particular, were characterized by a clearness of enunciation that bespoke an efficient training and successful study of mnemonical principles . . .'

Another aspect of Jezreel's versatility was revealed by his amazingly shrewd and practical flair for business. Converts soon began to arrive in Gillingham from abroad, having sold up and chosen to leave their homes in order to be with the 'Messenger' when the last watch drew to its end, and the ingathering of Israel took place. Jezreel did not insist, as Wroe had done, that his male followers should be circumcised and wear a distinctive dress. He did ordain, however, that they should let their hair grow long, and this was normally done up in a roll at the back of the head, and worn under a velvet cloth cap or, indoors, under a round purple cap which resembled a smoking cap minus the tassel.

Many of the converts put all their money in a central fund or 'treasury' administered by Jezreel; thus the 'Messenger' had to devise some means of providing these followers with a means of gaining their living. Partly with this end in view, but also because he was a clearheaded businessman, who wanted to establish the 'New and Latter House of Israel' on a sound and lasting economic basis, Jezreel started a number of shops in Chatham and Gillingham. These were all under his personal proprietorship, and he spared no expense in advertising them. The following, taken from the *Chatham and Rochester Observer* of Saturday, October 18, 1884, is typical:

'Important to the Inhabitants of Chatham,
New Brompton, and Maidstone.

THE NEW GERMAN BAKERY,
42 Luton Road, Chatham,
Proprietor: MR. JAS. J. JEZREEL.

This establishment has been opened for the purpose of supplying the inhabitants and gentry of this district with

PURE BREAD.

Perfect cleanliness is guaranteed in the process of kneading, baking, etc. None but the best and most skilled workmen in this branch are allowed to handle the same. None but the purest of flour is used in the bakery, thereby assuring that which is so essential to food health.
The 'Staff of Life' for the Poor, as well as for the Rich, at prices merely to pay the cost of production.
Bread will be delivered daily, by parties giving or sending their orders. All orders by post will be promptly attended to.

TERMS — STRICTLY CASH.'

Another of Jezreel's shops was a grocery and provision store in Railway Street, Gillingham, which was opened on November 22, 1884. An advertisement in the *Chatham and Rochester Observer* on Saturday, November 15, 1884 said:

'The leading principles of this establishment will be the providing, for the public good, the best and purest articles of consumption at the lowest possible marginal profit; purity and quality always being the leading features . . . I purposely abstain from the sensational style of advertising, so prevalent in these days of keen competition, but simply advise all householders who study ECONOMY to examine my prices with the quality offered, and so judge for themselves. . . . All the provisions are guaranteed of the best and soundest quality.

MY TERMS ARE STRICTLY CASH.'

JEZREEL.

WHOLESALE AND RETAIL PROVISION AND TEA MERCHANT.

154 & 156, HIGH STREET, NEW BROMPTON.

LONDON BRANCH:

126, GREAT TITCHFIELD STREET, W.

Great care is taken in the selecting and blending of the following teas:—

Good sound useful Tea	1/8 and 1/10 per lb.	
Choice blend of India and China Teas	2/- per lb.	3lbs. for 5/6.
Very finest blend of Teas	2/6 „ 3 „ 7/-	
Finest Pekoe Souchong of unusual strength	2/8 „ 3 „ 7/8.	

Fruiterer, Greengrocer, &c.,

21, UPPER MARYLEBONE STREET, PORTLAND PLACE, LONDON, W.

Finest English and Foreign fruits. Vegetables fresh daily. Coals supplied at wharf prices by the ton or cwt.

CARPENTER, JOINER AND WHEELWRIGHT,

CHATHAM HILL.

Turning, band-sawing and morticing machines on hire by the hour or day. Jobbing and contract work done efficiently and economically.

BOOT AND SHOE MANUFACTURER,

24, HIGH STREET, NEW BROMPTON.

A choice assortment of ladies, gents and childrens boots and shoes at lowest prices. A trial respectfully solicited. Repairs done on the premises.

PRINTER,

CHATHAM HILL.

Lithographic and Letterpress printing in all its branches. Stereotyping and Electrotyping carefully done. Machine ruling and Book-binding executed with promptitude.

PURVEYOR OF MILK AND BUTTER,

BEACON COURT, NEW BROMPTON.

Pure butter, cream and milk delivered daily within the districts of New Brompton, Chatham and Gillingham. Orders received at any of Jezreel's Stores.

SHOEING AND GENERAL BLACKSMITH,

CHATHAM HILL.

Agricultural Implement Maker. Horse Shoeing, &c. Jobbing in all its branches. Ploughs, Zig-zag, Chain, and all sorts of harrows.

GERMAN BAKERY,

42, LUTON ROAD, CHATHAM.

Familes supplied daily with pure home.made bread. Cakes and pastry to order.

ONCE USED. ALWAYS USED.

JEZREEL'S MAGIC POLISH?

An Excellent Furniture Cream, which will be welcomed by all cleanly housekeepers.

It requires but little labour

AND IMPARTS A BEAUTIFUL FINISH TO ALL ARTICLES OF FURNITURE.

Try a bottle and you will never be without it.—To.be obtained at any of JEZREEL'S Establishments, or through any respectable tradesman.

Prices, 6d., 9d. and 1s. per bottle.

THE JEZREEL TRADING CONCERNS

(From *The Messenger of Wisdom and Israel's Guide*)

34

Some little while later Jezreel's secretary enlarged on the conception of 'purity' which was so prominently featured in the
advertisements. Speaking to a correspondent of the London
newspaper the *Standard*, he remarked, with complacent pride:

'We expect numerous families to arrive daily from all parts of the
world. We have taken a large number of houses and opened shops, in
, order that we may supply them with pure food. Purity is our aim:
purity of food, purity of life, purity in everything. The outside public
may come and buy at our shops if they choose. . . . '

In addition to the German Bakery and the Grocery and Provision Stores, a dairy farm was run near to 'Woodlands', and
restaurant and refreshment rooms, a watchmaker's, a carpenters'
and joiner's shop, a smithy, a boot and shoe shop, and a printing
establishment, were all in due course set up in Chatham and
Gillingham. These businesses were managed under Jezreel's
supervision by members of the sect, who received a fixed wage
from which contributions to the treasury were deducted in
advance. These contributions, and those coming from believers
in other parts of Britain and the world, together with the profits
made from the various business ventures, soon amounted to a
considerable sum.

Jezreel did not fritter these away. He invested them prudently,
but only for the time being. As the fortunes of the 'New and
Latter House of Israel' prospered, so his ambitions developed. By
the end of 1884 he felt that the financial position was strong
enough to enable him to embark on his most cherished project.
This was the erection of an enormous square building which
should serve as both sanctuary and headquarters for the faithful,
and be, in effect, a visible rallying-point for the 144,000 who were
to be the immortal bride of Christ.

IV

ISRAEL'S SANCTUARY

THE manner in which the site of the building, afterwards known as 'Jezreel's Tower', came to be chosen was, according to Jezreel's own account, as follows. One night he had a revelation from God, and as a result woke up shortly after daybreak. Having dressed, he walked along the footpath leading from 'Woodlands' to the top of Chatham Hill. He walked on until he came to the highest point, from which to the north a magnificent view extended over the Medway estuary and the North Sea, whilst to the south lay undulating, wooded Kentish countryside as far as the eye could see.

Here, Jezreel believed, was the preordained site for the building which he envisaged. This was to be based on Revelation xxi, 16:

'And the city lieth foursquare, and the length is as large as the breadth... The length and the breadth and the height of it are equal...'

The building was to serve as sanctuary, assembly hall and general headquarters of the 'New and Latter House of Israel'; so Jezreel wished to acquire a site several acres in extent, which would enable ancillary establishments, like Jezreel shops, to be erected around the perimeter. When he made inquiries about the site which he had in mind difficulties arose, however. These, his secretary stated later, proved 'insurmountable'; [and though it is now impossible to verify the facts, it seems that objections may have come from the War Office. Jezreel's chosen site was not far from Fort Darland, one of the ring of forts around the Medway Towns constructed after the Crimean War, and the army authorities probably objected that the erection of a high tower would interfere with the field of fire from the fort, the construction of which was being envisaged at this time.

Whatever the reason, Jezreel had reluctantly to abandon his first choice of site, and accept an offer of six and a quarter acres of land several hundred yards nearer the top of Chatham Hill. He paid an estate development company (the 'Rock Freehold Land Society') £2,700 for it, and as soon as the transaction was completed, he engaged Messrs. Margetts of Chatham, a well-known firm of architects, to draw up the plans of the building which he wished to be erected.

His main desire was that it should be a perfect cube, each side of which was to be 144 feet (the mystical number!) in length. After much argument the architects convinced him that this design was impracticable, both for technical reasons, and on grounds of cost. In the end therefore Jezreel had to accept a modified version of the building he envisaged, and as finally determined, each side was to be 124 feet 6 inches, and the height at the corners 120 feet. In all other respects Messrs. Margetts tried faithfully to carry out Jezreel's own far-reaching ideas, many of which were original and far in advance of his time. The following description of the plans for the building is based in information given by the architects to the *Chatham and Rochester Observer* on July 4, 1885.

The structure was to be built of steel and concrete with yellow brick walls, and eight castellated towers of the same material. On each side of the outer walls emblems and symbols of the 'New and Latter House of Israel' were to be portrayed in stone, standing out in bold relief. Chief of these were the Trumpet and the Flying Roll, the Crossed Swords of the Spirit, and the Prince of Wales Feathers, signifying the Trinity. A large basement was to be constructed for storage purposes, machinery for working lifts, heating apparatus etc. Above the basement the entire ground floor was to be used for twelve large printing presses, designed to turn out thousands of copies of the *Flying Roll* and other literature of the sect.

Above the ground floor there was to be the Assembly Room, which was undoubtedly Jezreel's finest and most original conception. It was to be circular in shape like an amphitheatre, was

D 37

to reach almost to the top of the building, and was to accommodate 5,000 people. In the roof of this great room or hall there was
to be a glass dome, 94 feet in diameter, and invisible from outside
the building. The dome, supported by twelve massive steel ribs,
was to rise 100 feet above the floor, and in the dome a revolving
electric lantern 45 feet in diameter was to be the source of light,
since the Assembly Room was not to have any windows. Under
the dome three circular galleries or balconies were to supplement
the seating accommodation on the main floor. The curved space
between the dome and the outer walls was to be used, on three
floors, to provide offices, reading rooms, and other requirements
of a headquarters building.

The tower was to embody a number of remarkable features.
Chief of these, perhaps, was the circular platform in the centre of
the floor of the Assembly Room. It was to be 24 feet in diameter,
and capable of being raised by hydraulic pressure to a height of
30 feet. It was to accommodate the choir, and the preachers, and
was to be made to rotate slowly so that each part of the congregation in the vast circular hall could be faced in turn.

All doors in the building were to be made to open outwards,
to ensure swift and orderly evacuation of the premises in case of
fire. Jezreel tried to guard against such a calamity, however, by
insisting that the tower should be made as fireproof as possible
by extensive use of non-combustible materials such as steel,
concrete, and brick.

From the outside, the first floor of the building (the floor of the
Assembly Room) was to be approached by eight flights of steps,
each pair leading to a main door in the centre of each front. The
offices and other apartments in the upper floors of the building,
between the dome and the outer walls, were to be reached by
means of staircases in three of the four castellated corner towers,
and by a lift in the other. Gas and electric light were both to be
used for lighting, and – a remarkable innovation for the time –
Jezreel made plans for the towers at the corners to be illuminated
with electric lights on special occasions.

The roof of the building surmounting the dome was to be flat,

ISRAEL'S SANCTUARY

The Tower as it would have looked if completed.

(From *The Messenger of Wisdom and Israel's Guide*)

unkind tilt at the 'New and Latter House of Israel' aroused Jezreel's wrath. He threatened to sue the *Standard* for libel; but at length he consented to a settlement out of court, the main feature of which was that the *Standard* undertook to publish a long article by Jezreel setting out the beliefs of the 'New and Latter House of Israel'.

The extraordinary combination of religious fervour and business acumen in Jezreel was displayed in the letters which he sent to members of his flock, asking them to sell up their possessions and come to help in the building of the sanctuary and headquarters. In July 1884 he is said to have sent a long letter to some of the brethren in the United States, saying that the Immortal Spirit had revealed to him that it was the Lord's will that the brethren should 'settle up their affairs', and then come with their wives and children to Gillingham.[1] The letter continued:

'The above-mentioned members will settle their affairs as speedily as possible, yet as profitably as they can. They are not to drop everything at once, nor yet to sacrifice anything, but to sell out to the very best advantage, that they may do all in their power to bring over with them as much money as they can, to enable us to put up the steam printing-press and the large building 144 feet square. . . . Once this is up, the work will be spread all over the world like lightning. No one must bring furniture or cumbersome luggage with them. But let all convert everything into gold, and bring all they can with them in the way of cash, but no more luggage than is necessary. All these things will be provided for them here (Gillingham) when they arrive. I want to commence the building and put up the steam press by the 1st September! The whole must be completed by the first of January 1885, ready for the grand jubilee. *I must have ten thousand pounds* to accomplish all the Lord requires me to do. He has given me the order to commence the building by that time, and I am sure he will find the means.

As soon as the building is completed and the steam printing-press is up I shall send for all the members to come over, for by that time I shall have employment for all, male, and female, and children. Inform

[1] What was stated to be a copy of this letter was later reproduced in the *Chatham and Rochester News* of July 14, 1888.

all bodies in America and Canada that the building must go up on the 1st of September, and must be built ready to receive members by the jubilee of 1885, that *all* in England, Scotland and America may be present! Hence it is necessary now to send forth the great proclamation through the length and breadth of the land, for every true Israelite in America to try and have a stone in the building, for their own eternal glory. Ever remember the royal law of Christ, that true virtue is the sacrifice of self for the benefit of others!

Israel must now be gathered. This grand jubilee in January must be held in our own temple – all must be ready by that time. No one will have cause to regret what they have given to the building, and the press, which shall turn the world upside down! . . . The *Roll* will now be printed as John Wroe saw it:

"A large engine working night and day,
Throwing off great pack sheets."

I am looking out for several large farms, and hope soon to lease them for a few years, that I may find profitable employment for all Israel. . . . Hear, O House of Israel! The time has now come for each one to be put to the test, to see whether they love gold, silver, or land, or house, more than the bones of my body, my bride, my church, saith the Lord. . . .

All help me by every means in their power to get up the building. . . . It is to be the grandest building in the whole of these parts. . . . The whole House of Israel is now shortly to be brought in; work will be found for all; and we shall all be one fold, one cup, one body, whose head is Christ!'

Jezreel's stirring words and glowing promises had the desired effect on the faithful. Men and women and children began to arrive in Gillingham from other parts of Britain, and abroad, to play their part in the great work. Jezreel's wildly optimistic hope that the sanctuary would be completed by January 1885 was, however, far from fulfilled. Only the foundations and the basement had been completed by then; and two months later the entire project was halted by a calamity which none of the faithful had thought possible. Jezreel, the 'Stranger', the 'Messenger', the 'Trumpeter' and 'Ingatherer of Israel', died!

41

V

THE TRUMPETER DEPARTS

THE news of Jezreel's death may have come as a shock and surprise to most of his followers, but some at least were not unprepared for the news. In January 1885 he burst a blood-vessel, and though he recovered and was able to resume his activities for a short while, he fell ill once more in February, and from then onwards was not seen again in public. On Sunday, March 1, 1885, he burst another blood-vessel, and died shortly afterwards. A person who saw the body a day after Jezreel's death gave the following description, published in the *Chatham and Rochester Observer* on March 7:

'The room in which the deceased was lying was a well-furnished bedroom containing several windows, through which the sun shone brightly. The body lay on an iron Arabian bedstead, and at first sight it appeared as if the deceased had simply fallen back exhausted, and was in a deep sleep. He was lying on his back, with his head slightly on one side, his light flowing locks clustering over his shoulders, while his beard came down to his breast. His eyes were carefully closed, and altogether he presented a pleasing appearance. One thing I could not fail to notice was his massive build; he must have measured two feet across the shoulders, and was nearly six feet in height . . .'

The funeral took place in Grange Road Cemetery, next to the ancient parish churchyard of Gillingham, at noon on Thursday, March 5. In accordance with their custom, the members of the 'New and Latter House of Israel' indulged in none of the conventional manifestations of mourning, and, in the words of an onlooker, 'seemed from first to last to treat the matter with great indifference'. This seeming indifference however merely reflected the belief of members of the sect that to show any sign of grief would be tantamount to expressing a fear that the future of the departed 'Messenger' was not assured.

In the lane outside 'Woodlands' a hearse, two coaches, and Jezreel's own private carriage were drawn up, watched by a few curious country lads standing by the entrance drive. In the grounds of the house several young women members of the sect watched with equal curiosity as the coffin was put in the hearse. Next, twelve of the late leader's followers, all men, climbed into the carriages, which without any further ado set off for Grange Road Cemetery, some little way down Woodlands Lane.

The Burial Board, because it feared that the large crowd which had collected might cause damage, had closed the cemetery to the public, and this caused much grumbling and dissatisfaction. The spectators were however determined to satisfy their curiosity as far as they could, and they thronged the road outside the cemetery gate. It was estimated that as many as 4,000 people had assembled; and a number of vehicles, ranging from stylish carriages to decrepit brick-carts, added to the jam.

The crowd had collected, of course, in the hope of witnessing some strange and exotic burial service accompanied by mysterious rites. They missed little, however, by being excluded from the cemetery, for the service at the graveside proved to be both brief and conventional. After a way had been cleared through the crowd the coffin was carried from the hearse to the grave by six bearers, followed by the twelve members of the sect. At the grave the Reverend W. A. Smith, Curate of Gillingham Parish Church, took the short service, which was according to the rites of the Church of England. At last the moment came for the coffin to be lowered into the grave. It was of polished oak, with massive brass fittings, and bore a plate with the simple inscription: 'James Jershom Jezreel, aged 45 years.' As the coffin was lowered into the grave the twelve Jezreelites took, so the *Chatham and Rochester Observer* reported, 'a hasty look at it, and then silently departed'. This example was not followed by many of the inquisitive onlookers pressing against the cemetery railings, and it was not until late in the afternoon that the last of them reluctantly dispersed.

The persistence with which these people lingered outside the cemetery gates reflected the intense local interest and speculation which Jezreel's death had evoked. The event brought great profit to the two newspapers serving the district, and they reported huge sales, not only in all parts of Britain, but also in many places abroad. The *Chatham and Rochester Observer* stated, on March 14, 1885:

'The death of J. J. Jezreel, *alias* James White has been a nine days' wonder. On Saturday and Sunday little else was talked about wherever two or three were gathered together. You could hear snatches of conversation bearing upon the subject as you passed along the street, and in the clubs and workshops and usual places of resort it formed the staple of conversation . . .'

Inevitably, the papers made a great feature of 'disclosures' concerning the character of Jezreel, and the nature of the services of the 'New and Latter House of Israel' to which the public were not admitted. One or two damaging allegations were made about Jezreel's character, but no proof was ever forthcoming that they were true. The unfortunate Mrs. Head, whose little band of Christian-Israelites had left her high and dry when they seceded to Jezreel, naturally took advantage of the occasion of Jezreel's death to pay off some old scores, and placed herself unreservedly at the disposal of the reporters.

The *Chatham and Rochester Observer* published on March 7, 1885 an interview with her, during which she allowed her vindictiveness full play. After the secession, she declared, she had sent her husband along to the barracks which housed Jezreel's battalion, in order to question the sergeant-major about Jezreel's character. 'My husband', Mrs. Head stated primly, 'learned that White was a married man with a wife and two children, who were not recognized by the army authorities. . . .'

It must be said that this story should be regarded with the utmost suspicion, to say the very least, for no proof of it was ever produced. If there had been any truth in it, the worthy Mrs. Head would, one feels, have ensured at the time that it was given full publicity. As it was, no mention of it was made until Jezreel had died – no doubt, from a healthy respect for the law of libel.

More harmful to the sect than Mrs. Head's spiteful accusations was a letter which was printed in the *Chatham and Rochester Observer* of March 14, 1885, under the heading:

'A DESERTED FAMILY.
(By a Sufferer).

A gentleman whose name we prefer not to publish at present (said the editor) writes from Manchester:

'Our family have been terrible sufferers by this delusion. Our own father who some time ago held a good position here, basely left his wife and us his children. He threw up his situation last August to follow Jezreel, and here we are, his children, struggling to keep home and mother from poverty.

My dear sir, spare no means, as you are an Englishman and an honest man, to expose and denounce this terrible delusion in your paper. The clandestine underhand way these people have gone about their business, and the sorrow and misery they have caused, force me to write you this. . . .'

After this *cri de coeur* a letter from a soldier of the 4th Battalion of the Bedfordshire Regiment came as something of an anti-climax. Writing from Hertford on March 12, 1885, he declared that he had known Jezreel when the latter had served, as Private James White, with the 16th Foot in India.

'While we were stationed at Secunderabad', the writer said, 'he collected a number of the worst characters of the regiment and attempted to found a sect, but the idea fell through. He left the regiment for home at Calicut, on completion of six years; having been more admired by the men of this regiment for his cleverness than for his piety.'

It can be seen that nothing very harmful to the reputation of Jezreel emerged, despite all the attempted muck-raking. Indeed, from interviews which reporters had with members and non-members of the sect, it became clear that the departed leader had been held in high esteem by many people. Non-members who had had business dealings with him described him as sharp and keen to drive a bargain, but always prepared to buy and sell at a fair price. Members of the sect, naturally, extolled the 'Messenger' both for his spiritual and his earthly qualities.

'I believe in the truth of Mr. Jezreel,' one member told a reporter of the *Chatham and Rochester Observer* on March 14, 1885, 'I have seen him several times, and had conversation with him; and I believe him to have been a good man – a thoroughly good man, a business man, and up to his work!'

Another member indignantly refuted allegations that Jezreel had claimed to be immortal, and had required his followers to pay homage to him. Jezreel, he said, had always told his followers:

'I don't say I am going to put on immortality; I cannot tell. But of this I am convinced, that there are an elect people. . . .'

Again, Jezreel had never assumed to be more than any other member, except that:

'He was God's Messenger, like a man handing you a letter of importance. It is the news that concerns you, not the man or the name he bears!'

Though Jezreel's private character emerged on the whole unscathed from the post-mortem in the Press, a good deal of unpleasant publicity was shed on the private services of the sect. The information came from ex-members, who for some reason or other had abandoned the faith, or had been rejected before they had completed all the stages of initiation. It is likely therefore that the tales which they told to the newspaper reporters were exaggerated, or given a malicious twist. On the other hand the various accounts from different sources have a good deal in common, and they probably shed as much light as can ever be hoped for on matters about which members of the sect were extremely reticent.

The *Chatham and Rochester Observer* of March 14, 1885 published a statement by an ex-member of the sect in which he declared that having received several 'pressing invitations' to join the 'New and Latter House of Israel', he finally decided to take that step. So, he went on,

'It was one Friday night that I attended the service in the Iron Hall, New Brompton. (The meeting place at the junction of Napier Road and Nelson Road, Gillingham.) Inside the building the "saints" were sitting in the chairs, and as soon as the meeting was declared open, several girls who are designated "virgins" proceeded to wash the feet of the "saints", the towels as they were used being laid upon the arm of Jezreel, and he walked about as if he were a veritable king. He had a small iron rod in his hand, and a bunch of keys, called "Peter's Keys", on one of his fingers, and all the members seemed to be afraid of him. Prior to my being made a member Jezreel asked me several questions, one of which was:
"Do you wish to come out of Babylon?"
To this the answer had to be given:
"I seek the immortal life!"
Jezreel then proceeded to give a lecture, stating most emphatically that he was the instrument used by God to call together the elect. This being concluded, a sword was taken down from the wall, where two were hanging, and handed to me. This I had to take hold of to typify the dividing of the soul from the spirit. The ceremony is termed "passing the first sword", and made me a part-member for six months, at the conclusion of which I would have to pass the "Second Sword". This was, I was informed, a far more trying ordeal . . .'

The ex-member said that he decided not to go on to the stage of the 'Second Sword' because he found out that no discussion was allowed.

'Jezreel's word was looked upon as law', he declared, 'and no one was allowed to open his lips against it. . . . He was the most tyrannical man I ever saw, and appeared to possess some kind of magnetic influence over his followers, who could never look him straight in the face, as his eye seemed to pierce one through and through . . .'

Perhaps it was not the alleged ban on discussion which deterred the convert from passing to the 'Second Sword'. Considerations of a more material kind may well have weighed with him, and tipped the balance. He told the reporter that if he had 'passed the "Second Sword" ' he would have had to hand his business over to Jezreel, dispose of all his books, pictures and ornaments, as these were not allowed; and finally, he would have had to contribute to the 'treasury' a tenth of all his future earnings. Moreover, the ex-member continued, when people passed the 'Second Sword' they had to write out a history of all their past life, detailing all the sins which they had committed, and the documents were handed over to Jezreel. He would read them, and afterwards tear them up into little pieces, which he scattered behind his back, to signify that the old sins had vanished, never to reappear.

Another description of a 'private service' of the sect was given to the Press by a Mr. E. B. Woodruff of Manchester, who described himself as an 'Anglo-Israelite', that is, one who believed that the British were the descendants of the lost ten tribes of Israel. At the beginning of 1882, he said, he attended by invitation what he described as 'the first great festivity' of the 'New and Latter House of Israel'.

He had to stoop when entering the meeting place, for two crossed swords were suspended over the doorway; and when he straightened up again he found himself in a room 'gaily decorated' as he put it, 'with mottoes Israelitish in character'. Four high seats, representing thrones, were at the corners of the room, and over each was a letter, N, S, E, and W, representing the four cardinal points. On two of these thrones 'virgins' of tender years were seated; of the other two, said the informant ungallantly, 'virgins (I beg pardon) of riper years in the persons of Mrs. Jezreel and Mrs. Rogers' were the occupants.

Jezreel was seated at a desk, and spent much of his time writing short messages on slips of paper. He placed these on a tray carried by a 'virgin', and she would take it to the designated recipient, who was then expected to rise and speak. From time to time Jezreel himself would rise and read from the writings of Joanna Southcott and John Wroe; and when he did this

'he grew very excited, his eyes protruded from their sockets, and he seemed greatly agitated . . .'

From time to time the service was enlivened by the singing of short hymns which Mrs. Jezreel accompanied on her harp; but whatever was going on, whether hymns were being sung, or somebody was 'preaching', or Jezreel was reading aloud, every quarter of an hour there was a short silence, initiated by the loud striking of a gong.

Occasionally Jezreel would transfer his short iron rod – the appurtenance of the prophet – to his wife, who was then considered to be under the influence of the 'Spirit'. Fortified by the symbol of authority, she read extracts from the *Flying Roll*, or quoted lengthy passages from memory, to the meeting.

In accordance with Jezreel's precepts, several of the younger 'virgins' were trained to speak at the meetings, and usually learnt their pieces by heart until they were word-perfect. Few of them, however, shared Mrs. Jezreel's gift for memorizing, or her self-assurance, and thus awkward pauses often occurred when the recipient of one of Jezreel's notes stood up, but then in confusion forgot what she was expected to say.

On the whole the accounts of the 'private' services given in the local Press were good-natured, even if they may have been distorted here and there in the interests of a 'good story'. One article, however, which appeared in the *Chatham and Rochester Observer* of November 21, 1885 was positively lurid. Under the dramatic heading:

'THE SECRET SERVICES EXPOSED'

it began:

'Divested of its mysteries and *indecencies* the tenets of the "New and Latter House of Israel" are . . . commercial speculations leavened with profanity. When I speak in terms so strong I speak advisedly, and emphatically, and so far as is compatible with the usages and customs of polite society, I will adduce evidence to substantiate my remarks . . .'

The only evidence which the writer could bring forward, however, were the hymns used at the services of the sect. These, he said, he made bold to stigmatize as 'lewd and libidinous'. Some of the hymns were printed in a little booklet of thirteen pages called *Songs of the Temple* (1885); and he quoted from the 'Sixth Song' the following verse, as a sample of the 'depravity' to which he referred:

'I will take my rod of pure brass,
And I'll bore thee through,
That corruption may from thee flow,
To be cleansed.'

Again, from the same 'song', verse 9:

'Man and Woman is My Temple,
They one Bride shall be,
'Tis the workmanship of My hands,
God – wo – man.'

And, the last two verses:

'Lo! The Virgin shall soon bring forth
A young *Prince* in flesh,
He shall reign upon His throne with
The Man – Child.

She shall bring to birth in *this watch*,
Deck'd in pure *white* robes,
I will give her pain, and strength for
My pure graft.'

The horror of the writer of the article in the *Chatham and Rochester Observer* was hardly justified. There can be no doubt whatever that the 'songs' were written in all sincerity, and obscenity and lasciviousness were, if present at all in the hymn-writer's mind, deep deep down in the sub-conscious. The real defects of the Jezreelite *'Songs of the Temple'* were their utter lack of charm, literary or otherwise. In all the annals of protestant sectarianism there can never have been written, surely, hymns of such utter banality and metrical raggedness. One example – admittedly one of the worst – must suffice:

'Wrestling, crying, cleanse our *blood*!
May Thy fruit appear in bud!
In our tears we see MUCH MUD.'

In all fairness, however, it must be said that in 1888 a larger collection of hymns was published, the standard of which was somewhat higher. Some of these hymns are of considerable interest for the light which they shed on the beliefs of the sect. Thus Hymn 75 begins:

'Six thousand years are nearly up,
The eleventh hour appears;
God's sword shall cause mankind to see,
Who are his lawful heirs.'

Hymn 232 states defiantly:

'Though unbelievers mock,
And vilify thy sheep,
We are that little flock,
Which thou, O Lord, wilt keep:
Thy recompense we know is here,
For our redemption draweth near!'

In true Christian-Israelite tradition Hymn 241 asserts:

'Oh England! Happy favour'd isle,
Where God's bless'd will is now revealed,
On which the God of Hosts doth smile,
Here God's elect will *first* be seal'd!'

When all allowances have been made, however, the verdict must be that the hymns of the 'New and Latter House of Israel' were, on the whole, sorry productions. It was just as well, therefore, that there were always harps, and violins, and piccolos, and – above all – uncritical enthusiastic singers, to drown the incoherence and crudity of the words in a torrent of sound.

VI

MOTHER OF ISRAEL

THE most pressing problem confronting the 'New and Latter House of Israel' after Jezreel's death was the question of who was to succeed him as leader. At first it seemed that the mantle would be assumed by James Cumming of Kilmarnock, Scotland, an elderly man who had been one of Jezreel's first and most devoted followers. Cumming was a successful preacher, and had also distinguished himself by publishing *The Scripture Looking Glass*, a work in which he explained the essentials of the Christian-Israelite faith.

When Jezreel died Cumming was making a preaching tour in the United States; but with a keen sense of the possibilities he at once broke off the tour and hastened back to Gillingham. Soon after his arrival the rumour spread that he had taken over the leadership of the sect; and colour was lent to this by the great publicity given to a grand public service of the 'New and Latter House of Israel' to be held in the Corn Exchange Rochester on Sunday evening, April 5 – for Cumming was advertised as the main speaker.

Local curiosity about Jezreel's successor drew hundreds of persons to the Corn Exchange, and long before the service was due to begin the place was packed with people, and many who could not get in were left surging about in the High Street. The crowd in the street was in fact so dense that police had to clear a way for Cumming, Mrs. Jezreel, and other notabilities of the sect, to enable them to reach the main entrance. They then found the Corn Exchange so crammed with people, even the gangways being packed with standing spectators, that Cumming, Mrs. Jezreel and the others had to go round to a side entrance, and get access to the platform in that way.

Mrs. Jezreel, the *Chatham and Rochester Observer* reported on April 11, 1885, was:

'modestly dressed in light attire, with an entire absence of the usual signs of widowhood'.

Mr. Cumming, the paper noted further,

'was a gentleman of tall stature, with a long flowing white beard, giving to him a venerable appearance. This was however greatly detracted from by the donning of the black skull cap worn by the Jezreelites'.

The service began with music by what was described as 'Israel's Band', consisting of a harmonium, violins, piccolos, and four harps, the latter being played, the *Chatham and Rochester Observer* commendingly noted, 'with some precision by four young ladies.'

Mr. Cumming then rose and addressed the audience. It was written, he said, that 'by their fruits ye shall know them'; so now the 'fruits of Israel's College' would be introduced. The first of the fruits was a little girl about twelve years old, who in a manner which revealed very careful preparation and rehearsal spoke for ten minutes on the text (Revelation xxi, 7), 'He that overcometh shall inherit all things'. The word 'overcome', the child assured her audience, was the 'germ of the Scriptures'. Only those who overcame would be blessed. The promise to them would be fulfilled at the end of 6,000 years, and it would be fulfilled to the 144,000 of God's Israel, who had had their blood cleansed.

A second child was understandably overcome by the occasion, and hardly spoke above a whisper. She said her piece bravely through to the end, nevertheless, taking as text Revelation xx, 6:

'Blessed and Holy is he that hath part in the first resurrection: on such the second death hath no power, but they shall be priests of God and of Christ, and shall reign with Him a thousand years.'

After this second little sermon had ended a portion of St. Matthew's Gospel was read, and two hymns were sung, and then the venerable Mr. Cumming arose to make the chief address of the evening. His theme was familiar. The Kingdom of God would be 'proved' at the end of 6,000 years, when the 144,000 of the lost tribes of Israel would 'stand with the Lamb and mount to Zion . . .'

Mr. Cumming began to elaborate on this theme with enthusiasm and considerable virtuosity; but the audience, so far very well behaved, soon showed signs of restlessness. At length one or two rude interruptions occurred; but Mr. Cumming, with the instinctive reaction of a practised campaigner, blithely ignored them, and quickly announced 'a little song', which turned out however to be a hymn of eight long verses and choruses. After this, Cumming sagely decided that the time had come to close the proceedings. Mr. Coupe, secretary of the 'New and Latter House of Israel', stood up and made the announcement, adding, before the congregation dispersed, that copies of the *Flying Roll* could be bought at the door for 1*s*. 6*d*. each. It was, he solemnly declared, God's last message to man, and was much wanted in these days. . . .

'The audience then dispersed slowly' (the *Chatham and Rochester Observer* reported), 'Israel's Band playing a voluntary the while, the *Flying Roll* being on sale without reference to the golden injunction "Remember the Sabbath Day, to keep it holy!" '

Mr. Cumming's venerable appearance, his ability as a preacher, his long and faithful service to the 'New and Latter House of Israel', his flair for publicity, his tactical expertise at meetings, failed to bring him the coveted leadership of the sect. All his solid qualifications proved unavailing in face of the brilliant personality, the sheer capacity, and the calculated ruthlessness of Mrs. Jezreel. The lady, also, was in a strong position since she as Jezreel's widow was privy to the inner administration and finances of the sect. Moreover she had had the great advantage of being on the spot at the time of Jezreel's death, and had used it to good effect. Thus when Cumming hurriedly returned from the United States it was to find Mrs. Jezreel already *de facto* in charge of affairs, and firmly determined to remain so. For a while Cumming tried to challenge her; but bitter scenes resulted which the old man could not bear. So, sadly, he left Gillingham, and finally returned to the United States, leaving Mrs. Jezreel in full and undisputed authority.

A contemporary wag (in *Notes and Queries* January 1887) remarked of Mrs. Jezreel's assumption of the leadership:

> 'Resigned unto the Heavenly Will,
> His wife keeps on the business still!'

Though no doubt the flippancy was rather cruel, the essential truth contained in the quip is not to be denied. Mrs. Jezreel was, above all else, a superb business-woman, and in her capacity for shrewd management of the sect's affairs she was in no wise inferior to her late husband.

As the widow of Jezreel she was made the administrator of his personal estate; but this was only £41 10s. 0d., and the formalities were soon settled. Much more complicated was the question of the land which Jezreel had bought at the top of Chatham Hill as the site for the sect's headquarters. There was, moreover, all the money which Jezreel had kept in the common 'treasury'. Mrs. Jezreel was informed by a solicitor whom she engaged to look into all these matters that the purchase-deeds of the land had not been properly executed. He advised that to put this and other matters on a legal basis trustees would have to be appointed to represent all the members of the sect. The solicitor also informed Mrs. Jezreel that if she, as head of the sect, wished to administer its property and assets herself, the law demanded that her authority for so doing should be given by the trustees as representing the members.

Mrs. Jezreel acted at once. She requested twelve members of the sect chosen by herself to attend at 'Woodlands' one evening. Here they dutifully listened while a lawyer read out a long legal document which constituted them as a body of trustees for the 'New and Latter House of Israel'. They signed the document at Mrs. Jezreel's request, and from then on they functioned as a democratic smoke-screen for Mrs. Jezreel's autocracy.

Since her marriage she had never used her Christian name Clarissa, and had always called herself Esther Jezreel. Gradually, as her power and pretensions developed, she became known locally as 'Queen Esther'; and though she always officially repudiated this title, it stuck to her for the rest of her life, and there is no reason to doubt that secretly, she felt rather flattered by it.

Certainly, she aped the airs and graces of a queen, both in the services of the sect, and in her appearances in public. At the services she would sometimes play the harp, on which she was an accomplished performer; and from time to time she would walk to and fro flourishing the prophetic iron rod, and reciting either from memory, or from the book itself, copious extracts from the *Flying Roll.*

Her stay with Miss Easton in New York had refined her, and had given her a polish which she had hitherto lacked. It had also given her expensive and sophisticated tastes which as the daughter of humble working-class parents, she had hitherto been unable to indulge. Once she had established herself as Jezreel's successor, however, she began to satisfy her desire to live in the grand style, without any inhibitions. She had an engagingly feminine weakness for fine clothes, and was always fashionably dressed. She loved, too, to drive around in style, and soon she was a familiar figure in the Medway Towns, seated in a handsome carriage, drawn by a fine pair of horses, driven by a Jezreelite groom.

Sometimes, prompted by her imperious and dynamic character, she took the reins herself, on one occasion at least with disastrous results, as the following report from the *Chatham and Rochester Observer* of December 26, 1885 shows:

'The Driving of Queen Esther.'

'Queen Esther, otherwise Mrs. Jezreel, the head of the "New and Latter House of Israel", will find driving an expensive pleasure if her experiences of Saturday night are often repeated. She was driving a pair of horses attached to a wagonette down the High Street of Chatham in a most careless fashion, and according to the evidence of an eye-witness, "as if she wanted to drive over everyone". Soon after passing Clover Street a barrow was knocked over, and immediately afterwards the wagonette came into collision with the tailboard of a van which was standing outside the premises of Mr. S. J. Hart, grocer. The force of the collision pushed Mr. Hart's horse through one of the windows of the shop, and the shafts through another, completely smashing the plate glass. The damage to the windows amounted to £15, while the horse was also injured. Queen Esther's horses and trap did not appear to be much damaged . . .'

Other unwelcome publicity was given to the 'New and Latter House of Israel' at this time by a scathing review of *Extracts from the Flying Roll* which appeared in the *Record*, a weekly publication representing the evangelical wing of the Church of England. The review, which appeared in the issue of December 11, 1885, said:

'It has been a dreary task to read them (the *Extracts*); they have all the inconsequence of dreams; they have no more "thread" than a dictionary; they have no foundation in fact as prophecy; and there is nothing to reward the toil of study but a strengthened sense of duty and a deepened pity for mankind. . . . No one can read ten pages of the *Flying Roll* without seeing that conceit and ignorance are a large part of the outfit of the author. The absurdities are legion; words are used regardless of meaning; texts are torn from their contexts; and whole paragraphs have as much consecutive meaning in them as the syllables of Abracadabra. . . . We deplore the appearance above the English horizon of this ill-omened organization (the "New and Latter House of Israel"). The Flying Roll of Zechariah was a moral message with holy sanctions, instinct with eternal justice; this *Flying Roll* is a Gnostic lucubration, intellectually feeble, morally worthless. . . .'

In addition to this magisterial denunciation, the *Record* also devoted a leading article to the sect. This was entitled 'The Old Foes in a New Face', and was even more scornful than the review:

'The Gnostics are upon us' (it began). 'The old foes have put on a new face. The language they speak is neither Greek of Antioch, nor Greek of Ephesus, nor Greek of Alexandria; it is English. English of the good county of Kent, the county of John Ball and plain speaking, the county credited with the invention of the awkward question:

"When Adam delved and Eve span,
Who was then the gentleman?"

57

Again the thoughts of men are directed to Adam and Eve. Again the challenge comes from Kent, but "the mad priest" of the fourteenth century was a pure-blooded Englishman and an honest Christian, a Socialist we fear, but with the best elements in him of Mr. Spurgeon and Joseph Arch. The new "mad priest" is, we guess, not an Englishman at all. There is an occidental twang in his idioms; moreover, he writes "rumors", "savors", "endeavors". But his idioms and his orthography are small matters compared with his pestilential doctrine. It continues in grotesque jumble almost every variety of Gnostic error; and in a strange tissue of absurdity, in which vulgarity is shot with ignorance, and verbs are in permanent disagreement with their nominative case, yet holding the Bible in its hands, it displays to the vexed and startled student a *Flying Roll* in which, it is claimed, God sends his message to men, before the end comes.

We have read the *Flying Roll*.

It has been dreary work.

Dante, had he wished to punish some heretic of his day, would gladly have assigned him for purgatorial penalty the perpetual companionship of the *Flying Roll*. . . .'

The *Record* ended its leading article by hinting darkly at sexual undertones of the faith propounded by Jezreel:

'There is an esoteric teaching, too, and from this we gather that, as sexual disorder was the great incident in the Fall, so, in some sort, the final healing of the body will turn upon the poles of sexual distinction and co-operation. That way, we think, the madness of this heresy lies. "Man cannot be completed without the woman." "As they agreed in the Fall, so must they agree for the Restoration."

These are hints, and there are plainer hints than these! . . .'

It says much for the character of Queen Esther, also for her sense of purpose and steadfastness, that in spite of the widespread condemnation to which the sect was now subjected, she went her way without faltering. Having achieved her primary aim, of securing the leadership, she next concentrated on completing the 'sanctuary' or headquarters. The fulminations of the *Record*, and of ecclesiastical notabilities like the Bishop of Rochester, and others, had little effect on the contributions to the 'New and Latter House of Israel', which continued to arrive in Gillingham in a steady, satisfactory stream from places as far away as the United States and Australia, as well as from all parts of Britain itself.

Some of the faithful made very large donations indeed. Among such benefactors was a widow, Mrs. Emma Cave. She was the daughter of a London undertaker, who had left her a considerable fortune. A great deal, if not most of this, Mrs. Cave put into the central 'treasury' of the 'New and Latter House of Israel'; and because of Mrs. Cave's generosity, and the self-sacrifice of other well-to-do members, Queen Esther was able to arrange for further work on the sanctuary to be done. Indeed, on September 19, 1885, the great day came when the corner-stone was officially laid.

The omens were inauspicious, for the weather could hardly have been worse. Rain fell heavily, and the wind blew in great gusts in a manner more befitting March than September. The flag of the sect strained at the halyards from the top of a lofty pole in the grounds surrounding the sanctuary; and nearby a large marquee flapped and pulled at the ropes securing it to the sodden ground.

Inside the marquee, on a wooden platform at one end sat Queen Esther, Mr. Coupe (the secretary of the sect), Joseph Head, and other leading members. Among the notabilities Mrs. Emma Cave was prominent, for to her had been accorded the honour of laying the foundation-stone of the sanctuary. The full contingent of pupils from Israel's International College was present, and created a highly favourable impression, as always, because of their smart appearance and happy smiling faces. The boys wore their grey red-braided uniform, and had their long hair neatly rolled-up at the back under their red-ribboned coloured straw hats. The girls too evoked much favourable comment because of their pleasing appearance. They wore the same kind of hat as the boys, but were dressed in becoming frocks of a light material, with broad red sashes. The total effect, it was agreed, was both festive and formal.

Israel's Band, comprising six young women playing harps, six boys playing violins, three playing piccolos, and a man playing the 'cello, and conducted on this special occasion by Mr. Chapman of the band of the Royal Engineers, opened the proceedings with a selection of music which lasted for half an hour. Amongst the items were 'The Barnyard Song', 'We have been friends together', and similar pieces. They made a considerable impression on the reporter of the *Chatham and Rochester News* who was present, for he wrote: 'More enchanting music I have never heard, and I was truly sorry when the sweet strains ceased!'

At the end of the musical selection the hymn 'Hark the Trump!' was sung, after which Mr. Coupe read passages from Scripture and commented on them. Addressing himself particularly to the visiting Gentiles, who had assembled to watch the ceremony from motives of mere curiosity, Mr. Coupe asserted grimly that they little recognized what lay at their very doors. They little knew the work which was now commenced in their very midst. Time, however, and a very short time at that, would prove all things, for the end was at hand. . . .

Following Mr. Coupe's gloomy prognostications another hymn, appropriately called 'Strike, Strike the Harp!' was sung; and then the assembly were asked to leave the marquee in orderly fashion, and walk to the spot nearby where Mrs. Emma Cave was to lay the corner-stone of the sanctuary. All eyes were on that lady as she left the marquee. The *Chatham and Rochester News* reporter stated that she was 'of comely appearance'; but then added, rather unkindly, 'she has seen over forty summers'. To make up for this unchivalrous statement, perhaps, he went on to remark that her face seemed 'always to be lighted up with a pleasant smile'; and then for good measure, and no doubt for the benefit of his feminine readers, he disclosed that she wore 'a rich dress of navy blue silk, with a neat bonnet to match, and a lace shawl, the latter being thrown carelessly round her shoulders'.

Mrs. Cave was preceded to the spot where the ceremony was to take place by a tiny Scots boy named Watson – a brother of the girl prodigies who so frequently preached at Israel's public services. Young Watson's father was a wealthy benefactor of the sect, so it is not uncharitable to assume that the choice of his son as page to Mrs. Cave, like the choice of the lady herself as the layer of the corner-stone, was a mark of recognition for services rendered. The little boy Watson, to quote the *Chatham and Rochester News,* was

'a little hop-o'-my-thumb, gorgeously arrayed in navy-blue velvet knee-breeches, tunic and cap, trimmed with silver braid';

and as he walked ahead of Mrs. Cave he bore on a crimson cushion a silver trowel, mallet, and spirit-level.

'Mr. Joshua Rogers' (to quote the *Chatham and Rochester News* again) 'a soulful-eyed gentleman of sallow complexion and jet-black hair and whiskers, who being a brother of Mrs. Jezreel is very *distingué,* walked immediately behind to see that the wind did not play any pranks with the articles in charge of the Lilliputian Israelite. Following came Mrs. Jezreel, looking supremely happy. She is a young woman under thirty years of age, I should say, with a cheerful winsome countenance, which is quite pleasant to look upon. . . . She had displayed considerable taste in her toilet, being attired in an elegant dress of dark green silk, with a white hat. She wore gold ear-rings, rings, and bracelets . . . all very neat.'

When everybody had assembled at the spot where the corner-stone was to be laid, a number of articles were first placed in a cavity inside the stone. These were a bottle inside which was a sheet of paper on which had been written a brief account of the ceremony and a list of the chief persons taking part; a copy of a local newspaper; and several coins. The cavity was sealed, and Mrs. Emma Cave, gallantly assisted by Mr. Margetts the architect, well and truly laid the corner-stone, wielding the silver trowel, mallet and spirit-level in workmanlike fashion. The stone was inscribed:

'This corner-stone was laid on the 19th day of September 1885 by Mrs. Emma Cave, on behalf of the 144,000. Revelation vii, 4.'

The ceremony over, Mr. Coupe called for three resounding cheers, after which Queen Esther presented to Mrs. Cave the silver trowel, mallet and spirit-level as a souvenir of the historic occasion. The richly-chased blade of the trowel bore the following inscription:

61

'This trowel was used by Mrs. Emma Cave on the occasion of laying the corner-stone of the sanctuary for the New and Latter House of Israel, the 19th day of September 1885, and presented by Esther J. J. Jezreel.'

Similar inscriptions were engraved on silver plates attached to the mallet and spirit-level.[1]

When the presentation of the trowel, mallet and spirit-level had taken place the company moved back into the marquee. A hymn was sung, and then Mr. Coupe once again addressed the assembly. He took as his theme the famous Southcottian text (Genesis xlix, 10) 'The sceptre shall not depart from Judah, nor a lawgiver from between his feet, until Shiloh come; and unto him shall the gathering of the people be.'

There were, said Mr. Coupe, seven connecting links in the chain of God's promises. These were Abraham, Isaac, Jacob, David, Jesus, 'the woman', and Shiloh. The woman was 'the woman clothed with the sun, and the moon under her feet, and upon her head a crown of twelve stars' spoken of in Revelation xii, 1. Even as the Jewish dispensation had ended, so would the present Christian dispensation end, and a new dispensation would begin. Shiloh, the child of 'the woman', would usher this in. Mr. Coupe did not, unfortunately, enlarge upon this theme, so it was left uncertain in the minds of his Gentile listeners, at least, whether he identified Joanna Southcott with 'the woman', or whether he believed Queen Esther had some connection with that mysterious being. Perhaps Mr. Coupe realized that this would be a disappointment, for he apologetically remarked that his lips were sealed on that particular topic.

He did assert, however, with complete conviction, that the persons who were present had, that day, seen the beginning of a wonderful change in the face of the earth. Shiloh, the disperser of confusion in modern Babylon, would shortly appear, and the

---

[1] The mallet, trowel and spirit-level, reposing on the original crimson velvet cushion carried by Master Watson, are still lovingly preserved under a Victorian glass dome by the widow of one of the last remaining members of the sect in Gillingham.

new heaven and the new earth would then begin. In time for that great consummation, Mr. Coupe assured his listeners, the people of Israel would be gathered from the uttermost ends of the world, and there would be joy unspeakable when they came together. He concluded with a reference to Jezreel. The Messenger, he said, had been delivering the message. Let the audience before him, Mr. Coupe, ponder well the truths and prophecies contained therein!

A Mr. Mihan, an elderly American convert whose long flowing white beard gave him the appearance of a biblical patriarch, stood up next and enlarged on Mr. Coupe's remarks. Israel's landmark, he declared, had been placed that day in Gillingham according to a divine plan which could be referred to in Revelation. The landmark stood four-square, its length, breadth and height were equal [sic!], and it could not be removed by the powers of Earth or Hell! This foursquare foundation was necessary, Mr. Mihan ended, to prepare for the redemption of the 144,000 of the tribes of Israel who had been sealed to reign with Christ during the millennium.

By the time Mr. Mihan had finished the service had lasted nearly four hours, and the audience, after such a barrage of apocalyptic fire, were understandably showing signs of exhaustion. It was just as well, therefore, that spirits were soothed, and the proceedings finally brought to an end, by a short musical selection by Israel's Band.

As the large congregation slowly filed from the marquee, Queen Esther was left surrounded by the faithful. She looked radiant, and she beamed upon them regally. The day had been for her a great, indeed a triumphant occasion. The sect was now, it seemed, so firmly established that a steady continuation of prosperity leading to the completion of the sanctuary could confidently be looked forward to.

Alas, however, for all those fond hopes! The prospect was fair only to deceive. Even during the few years remaining to Queen Esther dissensions were to develop; and these were but a prelude to decay and ultimate disaster.

VII

THE DISILLUSIONMENT OF
NOAH DREW

N OT many months after the laying of the corner-stone of the sanctuary, an event occurred which tarnished the hitherto unblemished reputation of the Jezreelites as a trading community. The story, reported in the columns of the *Chatham and Rochester Observer* on April 24, 1886, was as follows:

'SUMMONSING A DEAD MAN: THE JEZREELITES
AND THEIR BUSINESS'

'At the Rochester County Police Court on Tuesday, William Arnall, whose style of wearing his hair long at once proclaimed him to be a member of the "New and Latter House of Israel", or to use a more familiar term, Jezreelites, appeared to answer a summons for having in his possession, for use of trade, several unjust weights, at Gillingham, on the 24th of March.

'He pleaded guilty. Mr. J. I. Pope, Inspector of Weights and Measures, deposed to having examined the weights, and to have found a 2 lb, ½ lb and ¼ lb weight light. . . .

'Mr. Pope said the business was carried on under the name of J. J. Jezreel.

'The Clerk: "That puts us in a difficulty at once."

'The Inspector: "The defendant took the case upon himself."

'The Clerk: "He cannot take a criminal charge upon himself. You cannot summons a dead man. But still, the defendant pleads guilty, so I suppose the magistrate had better take a case."

'The Defendant: "I am the right man!"'

The Bench inflicted a fine of £1 with 9 shillings costs; and as the court made ready for the next case the clerk of the court, who evidently felt in very good form that day, remarked:

'They say Jezreel is coming back again; so perhaps the summons could have been left at the house!'

The prestige of the sect was further diminished in February 1887 as the result of trouble in which Queen Esther and Noah Drew were involved. Noah Drew had been converted by Queen Esther during her first missionary tour in the United States, but he had parted company with her and Jezreel because of disagreements during the second or 'covered-wagon' tour in 1882. Nevertheless Drew remained a staunch believer in the doctrines of the 'New and Latter House of Israel', and he soon patched up his differences with the leaders. Indeed, with all the enthusiasm of the repentant sinner, at Jezreel's bidding he sold up his farm in Michigan and came with his family to Gillingham in November 1884. Here, because of his fanatical faith in the 'Messenger', he paid all his money (said to amount to well over £1,000 – some accounts said £4,000) into the central 'treasury', and was happy in return to undertake farming work, and, after that, humble duties as night-watchman at 'Woodlands'.

Jezreel's early death came as a great shock to Drew, and this intimation of mortality shook the faith which he had so far held so fanatically. The veil, he said later, was lifted from his eyes; and from then onwards he stopped attending the services of the sect. Not only that, however, but Drew now tried to recover some, at least, of the monies which he had handed over to the sect. He obtained no satisfaction from personal interviews with Queen Esther, and so he instructed a solicitor to act for him. The solicitor wrote to Queen Esther requesting repayment of the money which Drew had contributed, but Queen Esther refused even to reply to the letter. For some reason or other Noah Drew declined to allow his solicitor to take the matter further, and the latter thereupon sent Drew his bill. Noah was quite unable to pay it; and so the solicitor tried to get Queen Esther to pay the account from the money belonging to Drew which now was part of the 'treasury'. Queen Esther, through the Trustees, refused to acknowledge herself as responsible for the debt incurred by Drew, and thereupon the solicitor applied for a writ, which was granted.

It was of course to be served on Queen Esther, but great difficulty was experienced in locating the lady, who proved to be very elusive. At length however she was run to earth in Chatham High Street, along which she was driving in a brougham, accompanied by Mrs. Emma Cave. Queen Esther, on the alert, noticed the solicitor's clerk coming up rapidly behind, and to avoid being served with the writ she ordered her coachman to drive on ahead as fast as he could. The proceedings now became farcical. The solicitor's clerk was not to be shaken off, and pursued the carriage along the High Street, and then along Military Road. He caught up with it at last, and handed the writ to one of the two ladies, whom he took to be Queen Esther. Then, breathing a sigh of relief he returned to the solicitor and reported that the job had been done.

The smile of satisfaction on the solicitor's face disappeared shortly afterwards, however, when the writ was returned to his office, together with a statement signed by Mrs. Cave certifying that it had been handed to her, and not to Mrs. Jezreel, and could not, therefore take effect. This move however proved useless, for the law took its course. Since Queen Esther had failed to pay the sum owed to the solicitor within the time stipulated in the writ, representatives of the Sheriff of Kent one day appeared at 'Woodlands', and after an unpleasant and hostile reception by several male members of the 'New and Latter House of Israel', seized some articles of furniture in payment of the debt said to be owed by Queen Esther.

Even now that redoubtable lady fought on. She instructed a solicitor to appeal against the court's judgement, and the execution of the writ. Meanwhile, full of spirit, she wrote a letter to the editor of the *Chatham and Rochester Observer* on February 19, 1887, in which she declared:

'Someone has been sufficiently kind to furnish for our entertainment a man from Gravesend, who, so far as I can understand it, is desirous on behalf of the Sheriff to extract from us a sum of money which is understood to be due to certain lawyers who have never furnished me with a bill or an account of any kind, and in point of fact have never informed me for what purpose they require the money.

'The man however in question is making himself very much at home. He is perfectly harmless, and is busily engaged in reading *Extracts from the Flying Roll*, in which he is truly interested. So that it is manifest the hand of God is plainly visible in all this; and we wish at all times to be willing to suffer (if unjustly, the greater the privilege) if only the will of our Father is accomplished thereby, and the chariot wheels of Israel are not hindered.

'The God of the Living will be quite sure to protect His own, and though it may not be His will to do so at present, yet sooner or later our enemies will be confounded and ashamed, for the promise is, "No weapon formed against Israel shall prosper".

I am,

Yours faithfully,

Esther Jezreel.'

Queen Esther's appeal was heard in the Court of Queen's Bench on Thursday, March 31, 1887. At the hearing it was stated that one Noah Drew, formerly a member of the 'New and Latter House of Israel', had been expelled, and had then asked Queen Esther to return certain sums of money, amounting to about £1,000, which, he claimed, he had been induced by 'fraudulent misrepresentations' to hand over to the sect. Queen Esther had refused to give back the money, but Drew would not take the matter to court. His solicitors, as he could not pay their fees, required Queen Esther to pay them from the money which Drew had contributed to the sect. This debt, however, Queen Esther refused to acknowledge.

Mr. Baron Huddleston, after hearing all the evidence, said that two questions arose. First, had the writ actually been served on the lady 'represented as the "Mother of Israel", or Mrs. Jezreel?' On the one hand there was the testimony of the writ-server, on the other that of Mrs. Jezreel, Mrs. Cave, and their coachman. It was true, Mr. Baron Huddleston continued, that people commit perjury to a greater extent than was commonly supposed; but he was not prepared to say that the three witnesses had done so in that case. The writ-server, with an anxious desire to get his business done, might well have too rapidly but quite honestly come to the conclusion that he had served the writ on Queen

Esther. He, Mr. Baron Huddleston, must believe the three witnesses, however; and therefore he came to the conclusion that the writ had not been properly served.

The question of attachment of goods within 'Woodlands' raised, however, another question. The 'New and Latter House of Israel' was a society entertaining strong religious views, and subscribing funds for the mutual support of those views. Then appeared a man, an outcast from the society, who told his solicitor that monies in the possession of the society were due to him, because they had been obtained from him in the first place by fraudulent representations. If that were true, Mr. Baron Huddleston observed, the monies in question could not lead to an action for the recovery of debt, but only for an action for damages. He was of opinion therefore that the order for execution of the writ must be set aside, and Noah Drew's solicitors must bear the costs of the appeal. Mr. Justice Smith concurred with the view of his learned colleague, and judgement was entered accordingly.

Queen Esther had triumphed; but she did not forgive Noah Drew and his wife for all the trouble they had caused her. The couple were made to live in a single room above the boot and shoe shop managed by John Rogers, an uncle of Queen Esther, in Gillingham High Street. Because they had no other means of existence than the charity extended by the sect, Drew and his wife had no alternative but to do as they were told. In June 1887 however they rebelled when they were ordered to move once again, this time to a small back-bedroom in a house in Mill Road, Gillingham, another property owned at that time by the 'New and Latter House of Israel' for the accommodation of its members.

Drew, who was now seventy, at last agreed to move to Mill Road provided that Queen Esther undertook to maintain him and his wife during the remaining years of their lives. Queen Esther refused, and on Saturday, June 11, 1887, Mr. Legg, the new secretary of the sect, sent Drew a letter informing him that at 11 a.m. that very day a conveyance would arrive outside the shop in Gillingham High Street to transport the Drews and their belongings to Mill Road. The desperate old man and his wife

68

took no notice of this letter, and then ensued scenes which the *Chatham and Rochester Observer* of June 18, 1887 chronicled under sensational headlines:

'THE JEZREELITES MOBBED
EXTRAORDINARY SCENE AT NEW BROMPTON
ATTACK ON JEZREELITE HOUSE
A FREE FIGHT
NOAH DREW IMPEACHES QUEEN ESTHER'

Because Noah Drew and his wife had refused to leave their lodging in the morning, as Queen Esther had arranged, a small group of Jezreelites, led by John Rogers and Mr. Maxwell, the schoolmaster of the 'International College', appeared outside their door in the afternoon, and attempted to make the old couple leave. They tried to force the door, but Noah had prudently locked it and had moreover erected a barricade of furniture behind it. The frustrated Jezreelites shouted angrily and hammered on the door, calling on Drew to unlock it and depart with his wife to Mill Road as he had been told to do.

The noise of these goings-on drew the attention of the neighbours and passers-by, some of whom collected in the back alley which lay behind the room in which Drew and his wife were besieged. The angry shouts of the Jezreelites had frightened Mrs. Drew, and she ran to the window of the room, and told the onlookers, in between her sobs, what the trouble was all about. Meanwhile, Drew himself in true frontiersman style stood guard over the door with his American hatchet in his hand. Maxwell, who had managed to get a duplicate key, unlocked the door, and by a concerted push the Jezreelites managed to push it open an inch or two. Maxwell was unwise enough to put his hand through the gap: but withdrew it smartly, with a howl of pain, when old Noah Drew rapped him over the knuckles with the back of the hatchet.

The Jezreelites had inserted a piece of wood between the door and the lintel, and they now began to use this as a lever to force the door open. The panic-stricken Mrs. Drew began to scream out 'Murder!' to the crowd in the alley outside; but Noah pounded the intrusive piece of wood to pieces with his hatchet. The skill and determination with which he wielded his formidable weapon had a sobering effect on the group of Jezreelites outside the door.

'They knew what kind of weapon it was', Noah Drew triumphantly told the newspaper reporters later, 'because I used to carry it when I was doing my rounds as night-watchman at "Woodlands"!'

The attack had lasted two hours by now, and the besiegers decided to withdraw, for the time being at least. Drew and his wife were left unmolested for the rest of the day, and during the night; and on Sunday morning kind neighbours helped the beleaguered old couple by handing up parcels of sandwiches and other food tied to the end of a long clothes-prop. A bucket of water was sent up in the same way, so that Drew and his wife were well-provisioned to withstand a continuation of the siege.

The Jezreelites had meanwhile been taking counsel among themselves, and at length John Rogers knocked on Drew's door and announced that they were prepared to make a compromise arrangement. They were willing to let Drew and his wife occupy the front, instead of the back room in the house in Mill Road, he said, provided Drew undertook to go quietly and as soon as possible. Drew consulted with his poor wife, who by now was almost in a state of collapse. Urged by her, he agreed to the Jezreelites' proposal, but made a further stipulation, which they were forced to accept, that the transfer should not take place until Monday.

Thus at last, on Monday morning, June 13, at half past eleven, the siege of No. 24 High Street, Gillingham, ended. In the presence of the police, who had been called to prevent any further disorder, Noah Drew unlocked the door of his room, his goods were loaded on a cart, and he and his wife then departed for the new lodging.

That was not, however, the end of the story. Some time later Drew happened to be walking along the High Street, when, at the junction with Arden Street, he noticed a small group of Jezreelites, including some of the 'infant prodigies', about to begin an open-air service. Still smarting from the treatment which he had recently received, Drew began to harangue the small group of spectators which had collected around the Jezreelites. The group rapidly grew into a small crowd, and someone obligingly fetched a chair from a neighbouring house for Drew to stand on. Mounting this, the old man continued his fiery denunciation of the 'New and Latter House of Israel', while the small group of proponents of the faith, a few yards away on the other side of the street, tried hard to look unconcerned and to carry on with their own meeting.

At last, however, one of them was provoked by Noah Drew's diatribes into answering back. This proved most unwise, for the sympathies of the crowd lay entirely with Drew. With one accord they tore into the Jezreelite meeting, ripped the 'banner of Israel' into pieces, damaged the musical instruments, and, crying out 'Who robbed the poor man of all his money?' they began assaulting the male Jezreelites, whose long hair soon came tumbling down during the mêlée. The members of the sect were outnumbered, and quickly beat a retreat, taking with them one of their number who had been knocked down, trampled upon, and pretty severely hurt. The temper of the mob was not assuaged however, and a few of the more vindictive went around to the alley at the back of John Rogers's shop, where they shouted abuse, and threw stones till every pane of glass in the house was shattered.

An urgent request was sent to Chatham for police reinforcements, and news of this soon trickled through to the demonstrators, who promptly dispersed. By the time Inspector Lacy and a posse of constables arrived from Chatham all was quiet; but the disorders of the day had so unnerved the local tradesmen that many of them shut up shop earlier than usual, and they feared that rioting would break out again once the police had departed. Their fears proved unfounded; but for days afterwards it was unwise for John Rogers or any of the other Jezreelites on his premises in the High Street to show their faces, for they were at once violently abused. Schoolboys, indeed, waited outside the shop for a chance to voice their opinions; and the persecution was such that the Jezreelites got no peace until they put up the shutters and closed the shop.

The odium which the 'New and Latter House of Israel' had drawn upon itself by its treatment of Noah Drew continued however to be gleefully exploited by the local Press. A reporter from the *Chatham and Rochester Observer* visited the old couple on June 18, 1887 at their new home in Mill Road, and this is what he said:

'Mr. Drew, who is a tall, spare man of elderly appearance . . . required but little persuasion to give a graphic account of the manner in which the disturbance had been brought about, and the undoubtedly cruel treatment he had received at the hands of those with whom he had placed the whole of his worldly substance.

I was at first shown into the front room, which was used both as a living-room and a bedroom, but in consequence of a female member of the "Church" being in the next room – presumably ill in bed – it was thought best that we (that is, Mr. and Mrs. Drew and myself) should adjourn to the kitchen, as the two rooms were separated only by folding doors, so that it would be easy for anyone in the backroom to have heard all that was said, if they liked to play the part of an eavesdropper.

However, before we had been seated long, and while my host was in the middle of his narrative, the member referred to entered the kitchen on some pretext, and although she must have observed that her room would be preferred to her company, she made no movement in the direction of the door, and so we were obliged to proceed back to the upstairs room. . . .'

After these rather unedifying manoeuvres had been completed, Noah Drew and his wife, bursting to tell their tale of woe, and still brimming over with a desire for vengeance, imparted to the reporter every possible scrap of information which they thought could be damaging to the 'New and Latter House of Israel'. Mrs. Drew, exercising the wifely prerogative, volubly

led off by describing in minute detail the hardships of the existence which, she alleged, her husband and herself had been forced
to lead in their back-sitter in the boot and shoe shop in Gillingham
High Street. The Rogers family, she declared, had given her and
her husband insufficient food, and poor food at that. As for the
Rogerses, they themselves had lived like lords. Why, Mrs. Drew
indignantly exclaimed, on one occasion she was about to put some
sugar in a cup, but Mrs. Rogers snatched it away. Mrs. Drew,
annoyed, had thereupon informed Mrs. Rogers that she, Mrs.
Drew, had just as much right to sugar as Mrs. Rogers had. More,
indeed; for whereas Mr. John Rogers had only contributed pence
to the 'Church', Noah Drew had given pounds. . . .

'After we came to Gillingham', Mrs. Drew went on vindictively,
'we found out the true character of James White, and found out what
this woman (Queen Esther) was doing, and what a despot she was.
Our eyes were opened gradually until we saw at last how it really was;
and so we came out for good, and we want to warn the public here,
and all over the world, against this religious insanity. . . .'

For some time Queen Esther allowed the Drews' accusations
to go unanswered. At last however, stung by the wide publicity
given to them, she published her own version of the story, in
letters to the national newspapers, and in an article in the *Messenger of Wisdom*, a weekly periodical which she had recently started.
In the article, she wrote:

'. . . As regards the case of Noah Drew, the Michigan farmer, who
has for some time past been airing his supposed grievances in various
papers – presuming doubtless upon our hitherto well-known refusal to
justify ourselves against false accusations – I need say little. The writer
is personally acquainted with this man's history and position of
respectability in America, having stayed for three months at his little
wooden cabin at Fleming, Michigan, occupied by his wife, himself and
their son and two daughters. It is reported that "he has been swindled
out of thousands". In the first place, he never had any thousands to
give! In letters to the late Mr. Jezreel he himself sought his advice,
asking him how he should act under his then embarrassing circumstances. In one of these letters he explained his pecuniary difficulties.

73

He had such a heavy mortgage on his farm, he wrote in 1882, that unless he sold at once to the best advantage he would be turned out on the street. Accordingly he did sell, and the small amount remaining in hand (about £400 at the outside) remained in his own possession, and was expended by him as he chose. I can truthfully say not one penny of Mr. Drew's money is invested in the building on Chatham Hill. Nevertheless, in spite of his many attempts to damage us and our cause, he has hitherto been maintained at the expense of the "New and Latter House of Israel". But how readily are lies believed, and how seldom is the truth sought for, and believed. . . .'

The *Chatham and Rochester News*, commenting on this apologia in its issue of November 19, 1887, remarked:

'If we remember aright, Noah Drew never stated that he had been "swindled out of thousands", but that he had given all he had possessed (about £1,000) to the late James Jershom Jezreel, who promised to keep him for the remainder of his life. "Esther" is very explicit in declaring that not one penny of Noah's money was invested in the building on Chatham Hill. We can quite believe that, as it probably went in assisting to maintain the establishment at the "Woodlands". . .'

Queen Esther's repudiation of various other allegations made against the sect in the national Press met with just as much scepticism. On October 1, 1887 the *Daily News* had published a long and critical article on the 'New and Latter House of Israel', to which Queen Esther replied at length a week later. She asserted that as far as she knew Jezreel's original name of James White was as likely to have been an assumed one as the name Jezreel itself was. 'James, the Servant of the Lord' as she called him, had never claimed to be Shiloh, nor had he ever declared himself to be the Immortal Spirit, and therefore immune from death. However, she added, the *Flying Roll* had come, through Jezreel, from the Immortal Spirit.

Reverting to herself for a moment, she asserted that never at any time had she proclaimed herself as 'Queen Esther', or 'The Mother of Israel'; but she then complacently stated that that had already been done for her in the first, second and third watches. Next she turned to much-publicized accounts of what was supposed to go on during Jezreelite services. 'Our time at the private meetings', she said, 'is not employed in washing "the saints' feet", or sounding gongs every quarter of an hour. . . .' She flatly denied allegations that members of the sect were required to get rid of all ornaments, pictures and books in their homes, and to surrender any private business to the sect.

'On no account', she indignantly ended her letter of refutation, 'is any encouragement given to any to divest their homes of libraries, pictures, ornaments, etc., or to deliver up possessions or businesses, and to trade only under licence from headquarters in the name of Jezreel. Quite the contrary . . .'

The *Daily News* was not impressed by Queen Esther's laboured denials. Referring to the statements in the original article which she had sought to disprove, the *Daily News* commented:

'Upon considering the authorities upon which those statements were made, we feel she is scarcely justified in her sweeping assertion, that "they are almost without exception wholly untrue". Most of the statements which she has now contradicted were made upon the authority of both past and present members of the "New and Latter House of Israel" . . .'

The *Daily News* ended its comments on Queen Esther's letter thus:

'Mrs. Jezreel states, with reference to the building at Chatham, that the members of the House of Israel are expecting at no distant date to see a similar-sized building erected in very many of the large cities of this land, to say nothing of the gigantic Temple yet to be reared, which is destined to exceed in magnificence even the Temple of Solomon's day!'

This reference to Jezreelite expectations reflected the unbounded confidence and optimism which pervaded the 'New and Latter House of Israel' at this time – 1887 – despite the unfavourable publicity which the sect had been given in the local and national Press. The feeling of strength and solidarity was due almost entirely to the dynamic personality and ambitious policy of Queen Esther. In such young yet capable hands the future of the sect might well have seemed, in 1887, assured for many years to come!

VIII

THE MESSENGER OF WISDOM AND ISRAEL'S GUIDE

ONE of Queen Esther's most successful ventures was the launching of a periodical devoted to explaining and spreading the doctrines of the 'New and Latter House of Israel'. This periodical she called *The Messenger of Wisdom and Israel's Guide*, and it was published, between blood-red covers, first as a monthly at 2d, then as a fortnightly, and finally as a weekly at 1d. The early success of the publication was undoubtedly due to the vigour and variety with which Queen Esther, its editress, endowed it.

No. 1 appeared on Saturday, January 15, 1887, and the opening words give a good indication of the unbounded self-assurance and unconstrained literary style of the editress:

'In presenting this the first issue of *The Messenger of Wisdom and Israel's Guide* to the public at home and abroad, we do so with mingled feelings of joy and regret. Of joy, inasmuch as it has pleased the Lord of Heaven and Earth to call and use us, unworthy as we are, as instruments in His hands of printing and publishing to the world the message of *Life*. . . . Of regret, because we are aware that in thus fulfilling our mission, which we know is of God, we shall be compelled to say many things in the cause of truth which will doubtless raise the wind of opposition, well knowing as we do that *truth* is never popular, though the *lie of a strong delusion* will be always so. . . .

'These pages will be set apart for the diffusion of knowledge as imparted to the earnest seeker after virtue, truth and holiness . . . and the subject of the message of the *Flying Roll* will be freely discussed. What we have to offer we give the public in language simple and plain, that "he who runs may read", and that a child can understand. The learned critic will doubtless in these pages find ample scope for amusement, and many a fault will be at once apparent to his practised eye . . .

76

but so long as our words are according to *truth* the earnest inquirer will heed none of *these* things.

If in conclusion ye find your hearts burn within you while reading these pages, depend upon it, it is because Christ is speaking to His disciples by the way . . .'

In a special article in the first issue Queen Esther described with disarming frankness her early life and her meeting with Jezreel:

'I was born in the year 1860 at Chatham Hill of very humble parents. . . . They sought to bring me up in the path of the Lord, but I disregarded all entreaties to give my heart to God, my heart was at enmity with God, I inwardly hated all that was good and holy, and loved the vanities of this present life. . . . This then was *my* spiritual condition about twelve years ago, until a circumstance took place which brought me to myself in a most remarkable and wonderful manner.

'A *stranger* whom I had never before seen came to my father's house about twelve years ago, and brought me a message of joy, peace and comfort. He drew back from before me curtain after curtain, revealing to my benighted mind the rich glories of the Kingdom of God. . . .'

Amongst 'Items of Information' printed on page 8 of the first issue, Queen Esther revealed that the old feud between her and her ousted rival, James Cumming was still alive:

'We take this opportunity' (she wrote) 'of mentioning that James Cumming of Langlands Street, Kilmarnock, is in no way connected with the "New and Latter House of Israel". Neither is he in a position to furnish any information whatever concerning the "New and Latter House of Israel" as he has advertised himself able to do.'

Subsequent issues of the *Messenger of Wisdom and Israel's Guide* conformed to a regular pattern. There were frequent contributions from children belonging to Israel's International College, for, as Queen Esther pointed out,

'It is written that "a little child shall lead them" (Isaiah xi, 6), therefore let us not be unwilling to receive instruction from children!'

To these juvenile efforts, dialogues, supposedly real, between

77

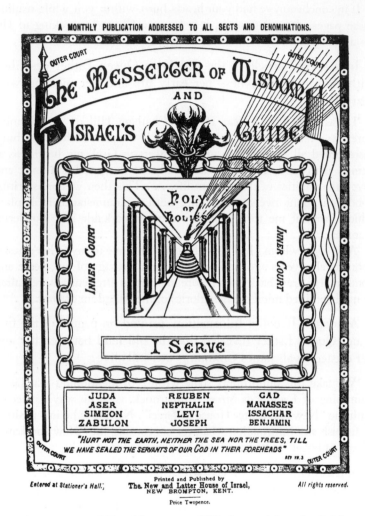

Front cover of *The Messenger of Wisdom and Israel's Guide.*

believers and would-be converts were added, also short stories
with such alluring titles as 'Laneside Cottage: or The Vicar and
The *Roll*', and letters to the editor signed 'lover of truth', and so
on. To add to the variety, and to keep the readers in suspense,
also (no doubt) to encourage them to subscribe to the next issue,
a serial story was run, with, of course, a proselytizing theme.

This literary assortment seems to have had a considerable
appeal, for in No. 3 of the *Messenger*, Queen Esther wrote:

'We are pleased to inform the members of the House of Israel that
the *Messenger of Wisdom and Israel's Guide* has been well received at
home and abroad. Some ten thousand copies of the first issue have
already been disposed of, and we feel sure that this number might
have been almost doubled if the members one and all had realized
their individual responsibility in the matter of its sale and circulation.
. . . Canvassers will find in many districts a wide field for their energies;
for many are the towns and villages where the work has as yet never
been heard of. . . .'

Apparently the response of the faithful to this call was not
sufficient to satisfy Queen Esther's relentless urge to expand the
circulation. In pursuit of this aim she did not scorn to enrol sales-
men and saleswomen on a purely businesslike basis, as the
following advertisement in No. 8 of the *Messenger* shows:

'WANTED: Respectable young men and women to sell religious
works on commission. Apply to manager, J.M. Printing Offices, New
and Latter House of Israel, New Brompton, Kent.'

Queen Esther also tried to make the *Messenger* self-supporting
by canvassing for advertisements. Despite her boast about the
circulation, however, few non-members of the sect placed
advertisements, and to make up the deficiency she advertised
extensively, in bold type, the various Jezreel trading concerns.
Undoubtedly many would-be 'Gentile' advertisers had received
Queen Esther's figure of 10,000 with a grain of salt, noting that
with her usual scrupulous regard for verbal accuracy she had
merely claimed that that number of copies of the first issue had
been 'disposed of'. This, they may have reasonably thought, did
not necessarily mean 'sold'.

In any case, however, as successive issues of the *Messenger* appeared, the complete authenticity of some articles and special features seemed open to doubt. Suspicions of this sort must have occurred to any readers whose critical faculties were not blunted, or in suspense, by membership of the sect.

For example, in No. 4, which appeared on April 15, 1887, there was a special article entitled 'My Life's Experiences'. The writer said:

'I had occasion one day – some four years ago now – to call the attention of a policeman, who was on duty outside my shop in Oxford Street, to a suspicious-looking parcel which had been left on my counter, and was supposed to be a package containing tea. Upon a careful examination I found sawdust trickling out of it, and knowing the many explosions of dynamite which had taken place in London and elsewhere, I felt considerably relieved when we ascertained that the contents of the parcel were quite harmless. This circumstance led however to an interesting conversation as to the unsettled state of affairs, and in fact the state of the world in general. We spoke about the signs of the time, and presently discussed the subject of the restoration of the lost tribes. This led to his introducing to my notice a copy of a book entitled *Extracts from the Flying Roll . . .*'

If this story of the unusual policeman seemed itself somewhat unusual, a letter which appeared in No. 5 of the *Messenger* on May 14, 1887, strained credulity rather more. It was said to be from an uneducated couple who sought guidance on the faith propagated by the 'New and Latter House of Israel'. The letter read as follows:

'Honord Madam,
    It aint no good at all talkin about doin a thin an never doin of the same so sais i i rites the day sartin for heres me an Betsy Jane a sittin thinkin over this ere book or yourn an lettin the tay git cold nite arter nite . . . if i ha made any blunders maybe youll scuse them for i baint no scollar and belave me mum your obadient sarvants
                                    Joseph and Betsy Jane Morgan
    PS. Enclosed fully directioned envelop for reply.'

Underneath this strange missive was printed Queen Esther's reply:

'We are glad that you received our letter of the 30th April safely, and that you are carefully reading the references in the *Roll* bearing upon the questions you ask in the above letter. – Editress.'

Queen Esther was indeed so captivated, seemingly, by the worthy couple's search after the truth that in No. 11 of the *Messenger*, published on November 15, 1887, she printed another letter, couched in the same curious style, signed 'your umble sarvant Joseph Morgan'. The editress explained:

'The following letter we print exactly as received, for the benefit of our numerous subscribers who so much appreciated the letter from these old people published in our May number. . . .'

As issue succeeded issue, the confidence of the editress grew, and soon she had no hesitation about airing her views on the international situation. In No. 13 of the *Messenger*, published on January 14, 1888, in her editorial headed, somewhat belatedly, 'The New Year', she wrote:

'The New Year has dawned upon us dull and gloomy. The European sky is overcast with black and ominous clouds which threaten a storm at no distant date. . . . No one will attempt to deny the fact that a tremendous conflict is inevitable. . . . While the temporal sword is being placed in the hands of the World to fulfil Scripture, the two-edged Sword of the Spirit is at the same time being placed in the hands of the House of Israel, also to fulfil Scripture. . . .'

Queen Esther shrank not, in the issue of April 14, 1888, from attacking the Reverend C. H. Spurgeon, the most eminent non-conformist preacher of the day. She tilted at him in an article entitled, with true Southcottian verve, 'The Rev. C. H. Spurgeon's new creed weighed in the balances and found wanting!' A few weeks later, in No. 18 of the *Messenger*, published on June 15, 1888, Queen Esther attacked the Church of England itself, in an article boldly headed:

'The 39 Articles of the Church of England compared with Scripture, proving the foundation to be on sand!'

Queen Esther did not allow her editorial activities to interfere with the many other duties which her position as head of the sect involved. Members were sent off on missionary tours, and they preached, often to hostile or ribald audiences, in provincial towns all over Britain. On October 11, 1885, for example, Mr. and Mrs. Mihan, two leading exponents of the faith, addressed meetings at the Alexandra Hall, Maidstone. Mr. Mihan declared (so the *Chatham and Rochester News* reported on October 17) that God's last message to man would be found in the *Extracts from the Flying Roll*, which revealed what the 'Spirit' had to say to the churches. All who had ears to hear *would* hear, and understand. The Gentiles however would refuse, and would trample the pearls under their feet. Israel on the other hand would hear, receive and accept, would 'eat up the little book' and be healed from the bite of the serpent, the dragon, and the devil. Then Israel would put on a change of raiment, and be ready to meet their Lord and Redeemer. . . .

In addition to the missionaries proper, scores of canvassers were sent out to sell the *Flying Roll* and the *Messenger of Wisdom* from door to door; and even Queen Esther's close relations were not spared this hard toil. Hannah Rogers, for example, was ordered to go to Scotland to gather converts there, and win subscribers to the publications of the sect. These plodding emissaries, continually spurred on by the indefatigable Queen Esther, scored some success, for by 1887 groups of the 'New and Latter House of Israel' were flourishing in London, Maidstone, Brighton, Lincoln, Holyhead, Ashton-under-Lyne, Kilmarnock and Glasgow, and the sect had even penetrated to St. Helier in the Channel Islands.

Missionaries were dispatched abroad too, and among these were Queen Esther's own brother Joshua and his wife, who were sent together to New Zealand to spread the faith in that distant land. By the end of 1887 they had worked so well that they were able to establish a flourishing group of converts at Christchurch in South Island. Other small communities were set up or developed in Detroit, Michigan, Vancouver Island, and one or two other places in the United States and Australia, so that Queen Esther was able in due course to claim, without undue exaggeration, that the faith was world-wide.

The converts, of course, were expected to send donations to the central treasury at Gillingham, and money from them did in fact flow in regularly. There were profits too from the various Jezreel trading concerns, and, perhaps, from the publications of the sect. Queen Esther was thus able to continue the building of Israel's Sanctuary, and by June 1887 the whole of the exterior of the immense tower had been completed, and only the roof remained to be put on. Inside the ground floor was finished, and already housed the steam printing machines which were incessantly at work turning out copies of the *Flying Roll*, the *Messenger of Wisdom*, and other publications.

Above the ground floor, through a bewildering mass of steel girders, which seemed to constitute one great tangle, the enormous meeting hall with its circular galleries and rotating preachers' platform could be seen to be taking shape. Not far from the sanctuary the Jezreel Smithy, occupying an advantageous position on the busy Watling Street, prospered exceedingly, as did the various shops and trading concerns which Jezreel had established.

Nor did Queen Esther, of course, neglect the spiritual propaganda which her husband had so cleverly spread through public services and meetings. She had a temporary hall built in the grounds of the Sanctuary, and here the members of the public were invited to attend every Sunday to hear good music played and the doctrines of Israel expounded by fresh-faced young boys and girls of the sect, or by long-bearded patriarchs and, naturally, by Queen Esther herself. The public *did* attend – although the excellent programme of music which Israel's Band could always be relied on to provide was almost certainly the main attraction.

A correspondent of the *Chatham and Rochester News*, who paid a visit to the hall on Sunday, July 31, 1887, found about a hundred members of the public attending the Jezreelites' evening service, though in intelligence and education, he remarked, he would class them as 'rather low'. Three young women were conducting the service, and behind them were harpists, violinists and flautists of Israel's Band. Next to them were the choir, dressed in grey uniform with red facings, and constituting, as always, a credit to Israel's International College, to which all the junior members belonged.

The sect was clearly under the control of an efficient and dynamic leader. She was young, too, and it seemed as the year 1887 ended and the new year began, that nothing could stop further steady expansion. Then, in the summer of 1888, a shattering blow fell. The sect, for a second time, lost its leader.

IX

DEATH OF QUEEN ESTHER

A T the end of May 1888 Queen Esther fell ill, but in accordance with her own wishes a doctor was not summoned,
even when her condition grew worse. Her face bore signs
of acute suffering, she lay silent and passive in her bed with her
hands crossed listlessly over her breast, and with her long hair
hanging loose over her shoulders. On the evening of Friday, June
29, she lost consciousness; and in the early hours of the next
morning she passed away, in the presence of her father Edward
Rogers and other relatives.

After some anxious consultation they decided that a doctor
must now be fetched, to forestall, if possible, unpleasant repercussions. So Francis Clark, Queen Esther's groom, and one of
her most faithful followers, was sent without further delay to
fetch Dr. Lamb, who lived in Gillingham High Street. The
doctor arrived at 'Woodlands' about four o'clock on Saturday
morning, and was shown into the bedroom where Queen Esther's
body lay. He found her relatives standing calmly by the bedside,
without any outward manifestation of grief, as was customary
with members of the sect when death took one of the faithful.
Dr. Lamb made a rapid preliminary examination of the body,
and then questioned members of Queen Esther's family and
household who had tended her since she fell ill. From their
answers he formed a tentative conclusion that she had died from
inflammation of the kidneys; and having said so, the doctor prepared to depart.

Edward Rogers, however, hoping to avoid the unpleasant
publicity following a *post-mortem* examination, leading perhaps
to an inquest, asked Dr. Lamb if he would, there and then, write
out a certificate giving the cause of death. Dr. Lamb refused, and,

moreover, considered it his duty to make a full report of the circumstances of the death to the local authority. Thereupon the coroner, Mr. W. J. Harris, asked Dr. Lamb to make an official *post-mortem* examination. The doctor arrived at 'Woodlands' at six o'clock on Saturday evening for this purpose, and as he was provided with the coroner's authority, Edward Rogers and his family were unable to prevent the examination from being made. This time Dr. Lamb diagnosed the cause of death as peritonitis, and as he further certified that it had occurred through natural causes, no inquest was held.

The circumstances of Queen Esther's death were quite prosaic; but largely owing to the habitual reticence of the Jezreelites the most fantastic and cruel rumours soon began to circulate. With the precedent established by Joanna Southcott in their minds, some people began to whisper that Queen Esther had taken to her bed because she believed she was about to give birth to Shiloh. As can be imagined, this theme lent itself easily to the most scandalous treatment and elaboration by the lewd-minded and the mischievous.

At length, to its credit, the *Chatham and Rochester News* in its issue of July 7, 1888, put a stop to the cruel rumours:

'There has been painful rumour afloat' (the paper said) 'reflecting on the character of the late Mrs. Jezreel, which we have never credited for one moment; and when, on her death being announced these were revived, we resolved to find out the truth.

For this purpose one of our representatives waited on Dr. Lamb on Tuesday. The doctor courteously expressed his willingness to answer all questions that he could, consistently with his duty.

Well then, had he heard of the painful rumour that was being whispered on a thousand tongues concerning Mrs. Jezreel?

"It is no use beating about the bush," replied the doctor, "let us come to the point at once! You refer to the story that she was *enceinte?*"

Our representative assented.

"Then," said the doctor, "you can tell the public on my authority that there is not a word of truth in it! It is a cruel thing that there should be such a report about, when there is not the slightest foundation for it!" '

In view of the tremendous interest excited locally by Queen Esther's death, the members of the sect did all they could to keep the date and the time of the burial service a secret until the very last moment. They let it be inferred, indeed, that the service would not take place until Saturday, July 7, so that members of the sect living in other parts of Britain would be able to attend. In fact, however, the funeral took place on Tuesday, July 3. As the secret had been very well kept, very few people were outside 'Woodlands' when, at a quarter past two in the afternoon, the coffin was borne from the house and placed in the hearse. There were only four mourners – and not one member of Queen Esther's family was among them. The four were male members of the sect: Mr. Legg, the secretary; Mr. Maxwell, the schoolmaster of Israel's International College; Mr. Clark, Queen Esther's groom; and Mr. Binder, her 'steward'. The four men all wore ordinary suits; and far from displaying any sign of mourning, they all wore gaily coloured ties.

They climbed into the coach which stood behind the hearse, and then the two vehicles set off down Woodlands Lane for Grange Road Cemetery, next to the churchyard of the old parish church. The weather was unseasonable. Gusts of wind and squalls of rain, with intermittent brief glimpses of sunshine, made the time of year seem more like March than July. The rain had turned Woodlands Lane into a muddy mess, with deep ruts in which quite large stones lay concealed. The two vehicles clattered and bumped their way along, and despite the foulness of the way, arrived at the cemetery gate on time.

The local authorities, remembering the tumultuous crowd which had gathered to witness the burial of Jezreel in 1885, had taken no chances. They posted Sergeant Chaney and two constables to keep order: but in the event this precaution proved hardly necessary, for only about a hundred people were present. Most of these were women; and among the men were a number of labourers from a nearby brickfield who had been stood off for the day because of the bad weather, and remained to watch the funeral because they had nothing else to do.

At the cemetery gate stood the Reverend W. A. Smith, curate of Gillingham Parish Church, who had buried Queen Esther's husband just over three years previously. He preceded the coffin, which was draped in a violet pall, to the grave, reciting as he did so the opening passages from the burial service according to the rites of the Church of England. A great deal of the remainder of the normal service was left out at the special request of the Jezreelites, and the four representatives of the sect stood impassively while the abbreviated service took its course.

They showed not the slightest sign of emotion as the coffin, of polished oak with brass fittings, was lowered into the grave,[1] and kept their hats on even at this most solemn moment of all. The coffin bore the simple inscription:

> Esther Jezreel
> Died 30 June 1888
> Aged 28 years.

As soon as the service was over the four Jezreelites hurried to their coach, and were driven back to 'Woodlands'. A *Chatham and Rochester News* reporter followed them, for he was curious to find out why no relative of Queen Esther had attended the funeral. At 'Woodlands' Mr. Edward Rogers consented to see him, and explained that there was nothing strange about the absence of the relatives. None of them had attended, he said, because they had 'arranged otherwise' among themselves; and with this question-begging explanation the reporter had to be satisfied. Before he left, however, he asked Edward Rogers one more favour. Would he describe the last moments of the deceased? Edward Rogers was quite willing to do this. 'They were glorious and happy!' he declared, and added with equal assurance, 'Her last words were full of hope!'

Edward Rogers may have thought that by pandering to some extent to the Press he might induce the local and national papers

[1] Esther was buried in her husband's grave. This is, by a curious coincidence, No. 1 in Row J. [Class B, of Section F.] Today the grave is a neglected spot, covered with long coarse grass, and with no memorial of any kind.

to keep strictly to verifiable facts when they printed accounts of Esther's career. If he did have any such hopes, they were sadly disappointed. Soon after Queen Esther had been committed to the grave a series of articles were published in the local papers; and these contained venomous attacks on the sect in general and Queen Esther and Jezreel in particular.

For example, in an editorial on Saturday, July 7, 1888, the *Chatham and Rochester News* stated:

'When a new edition of the "History of Religious Delusions" or "The Absurdities of Belief" is published, the story of the House of Israel will doubtless form one of the most striking chapters. . . . Queen Esther is dead. She will not be seen again in the streets of Chatham exhibiting her capability to manage a horse, or seated in her carriage with all the ease and grace of a duchess. . . . It is to be hoped that the Gillingham absurdity will no longer be continued to destroy the peace of families, seduce men from important, useful positions, and produce, as it has done, incalculable evil. There are men that had need to weep drops of blood that they ever listened to the overtures and pretensions of the man White, with his assumed name of Jezreel! Surely now, with the death of Mrs. Jezreel, no more dupes are to be caught! . . . Her name will be handed down as the propagator of fanatical absurdity!'

In an article in the same issue, the *Chatham and Rochester News* asserted:

'It was latterly the custom of "Queen Esther", Bible in one hand and sceptre in the other, to make her followers swear that they would never reveal the secrets of the House, and that if they were "cut off", or left, they would not claim back any money they had put into the treasury. . . . In one of the hymns of the sect we read:

The nations gifts do bring,
Unto the Queen and King,
And virgins without number sing.

No one can enter in
Unless passed by the Queen,
And trained by sceptre and rod.

There is no doubt that Queen Esther wielded the "sceptre" in the most autocratic fashion; though nominally the servant of Israel, she lorded it over all!'

The *Chatham and Rochester News* continued its revelations about the Jezreelites in its issue of July 14, under the heading 'Jezreelism in its true colours'.

'I am forbidden' (the "Special Correspondent" began dramatically) 'to disclose all that has fallen on my ears concerning a veritable "prison house" – the "House of Israel" – otherwise the Jezreelites' den. . . . The traveller who "fell among thieves" was not more completely "skinned" than he who cast in his lot with the Jezreelites, having previously cast in his purse. . . .'

The reporter went on to describe the case of a disillusioned former member of the sect whom he had visited at his home in Gillingham. This man had previously owned a thriving business which gave employment to twenty persons; but in 1881 a copy of the *Flying Roll* had come into his hands, and his thoughts were turned from business to religion. He wrote to Jezreel for information, and the latter not only supplied this, but also paid the man a personal visit. As a result he had become a fanatical follower of the 'Messenger'. Accordingly, when Jezreel ordered him, some eighteen months later, to sell up all his possessions and join the community at Gillingham, the faithful convert unhesitatingly obeyed. He sold his home, but kept the furniture, because Jezreel had told him that that was to be shared out among several families who had recently arrived in Gillingham from abroad. The business was sold at a 'sacrificial' price, because of the owner's wish to carry out Jezreel's order as quickly as possible: but even so, when he arrived in Gillingham he was able to give the 'Messenger' more than £1,000 to put in the treasury. In return Jezreel had allotted him, his wife and two children a house in Mill Road; and there the convert had lived, in much reduced circumstances, till he suddenly decided to have nothing more to do with the sect.

The reporter questioned this bitterly disillusioned man about several practices which, according to local rumour, had been prevalent in the 'New and Latter House of Israel'. The questions and answers were as follows:

'FLOGGING NUDE GIRLS.

The next question was put with a little hesitation, but the answer came sharp and clear.

"I know that girls were stripped by order of Mr. Jezreel in his presence, and flogged with a dog-whip for offences against discipline!"

"You are positive on this point?"

"Decidedly I am. My information was obtained from those who divested the girls of their clothing, from those who inflicted the punishment, and – and – from some who suffered the indignity. Their ages would vary from fourteen to sixteen."

"Did Mrs. Jezreel ever order a child to be flogged?"

"Yes – a little boy was stripped and flogged on one occasion until the blood ran down his back; but by some means the Society for the Protection of Women and Children got to hear of it, and an official came down. Nothing however came of it, as the boy's father had consented to the flogging, and actually witnessed it, as did Mrs. Jezreel – but she never attempted such a thing again!"

'MRS. JEZREEL PUT IN THE BLACK HOLE.

"Did you ever hear of a dark room or place of punishment?"

"There was such a place at Edina Cottage, also at "Woodlands", but the latter was a disused wine or beer store in the basement. Mrs. Jezreel was on one occasion seized and placed there for a day and a night, by her husband's orders. . . ."

"What was her offence?"

"I was told she was jealous of someone and had kicked up a shindy!"'

In search of more 'sensational disclosures' the reporter of the *Chatham and Rochester News* interviewed another ex-member of the sect; and this person seemed to be animated by a particular grudge against Queen Esther. She ruled the sect with a rod of iron, he said, and she was harsh and relentless towards anybody who offended her. She never forgave old Mr. Cumming for presuming to challenge her for the leadership of the sect after Jezreel's death. Thus, when in his later years Cumming became desperately poor, she refused to help him or even to repay any of the money which he had contributed to the treasury.

The reporter then asked:

' "What do you think of Mrs. Jezreel's action in keeping blood-hounds to terrify and frighten away from her domicile the poor and needy?"

"Why, sir," his informant replied, "I assure you that one of these savage brutes has even been chained to the outside gate of 'Wood-lands' to scare people from entering her grounds. . . . Her own post-man had a narrow escape. He was on horseback in the lane, and only saved himself by leaping from his horse. The latter fled for its life, pursued by the savage brute, which mangled the poor horse terribly!" '

The reporter next wanted to know the true facts about the 'virgins' or 'purifiers' of Israel, whose function at private meetings of the sect was said to be the washing and drying of the feet of persons who were admitted as full members.

' "Oh!" came the scornful reply; – "They were nothing more or less than the detectives! By eavesdropping and watching the move-ments of members they kept Mrs. Jezreel posted up in all that was said and done!" '

After two weeks of 'startling disclosures' and 'sensational revelations' the public appetite for information, preferably as lurid as possible, about the 'New and Latter House of Israel' was still unsated; and so on Saturday, July 21, the indefatigable *Chatham and Rochester News* produced yet another instalment of the saga, entitled, this time,

'THE JEZREELITE EXPOSURES: BY A "CUT-OFF" MEMBER'

This excommunicate declared that Queen Esther had several times been driven away from 'Woodlands' by her husband for trivial acts of so-called rebellion. Often the expulsion had occurred late at night, and Queen Esther had been forced to seek refuge in the houses of friends until she was restored to her husband's favour, and allowed to return to 'Woodlands'.

The informant also stated that punishment was meted out to the pupils of Israel's International College whenever they offended. They were forced to do out-of-door work, like chopping wood, or weeding, instead of normal lessons; were put on a diet of bread and water; and at night were forced to sleep in a wooden shed in the grounds.

The *Chatham and Rochester Observer*, not to be outdone by its local rival, also published a series of 'disclosures' about the sect, many of them repeating the allegations printed in the *News*, but some of them bringing forth fresh information. On July 7 the *Observer* published an interview with a local woman who claimed to have known Queen Esther when the latter was thirteen, and for many years thereafter. The woman declared that Esther had always seemed to be a selfish girl, and she had been very jealous, too, of her sister Lizzie. Jezreel had really preferred Lizzie to Esther; but Lizzie had died while Jezreel was in India, and so Esther had been able to step into her place.

After Jezreel's death, the woman continued, Queen Esther had proclaimed a month's 'self-denial' to be practised by all members of the sect. Only the plainest of food was to be eaten, and not much of that. Because the informant and her husband, and several other members of the sect refused to obey this order, they were 'cut off' or expelled by Queen Esther. (Another version of this story, published in the *Chatham and Rochester Observer* some years later, was that Queen Esther imposed the fast to enable £70 to be saved in one month to swell the treasury.)

The *Chatham and Rochester Observer* published in its issue of July 7 a long interview with a leading member of the sect, who was not named, under the heading:

A CHAT WITH A JEZREELITE CHIEF

This member was very critical with regard to the secrecy practised by Queen Esther in her administration of the finances. He was most indignant, however, about another feature of her regime which had already been given considerable publicity:

'"I object, and all along have objected, to the system introduced by Queen Esther of espionage and inquisitorial confessionals. The latter more especially. The written confessions of the members, male and female, from fourteen years upwards, which are read out before the

93

whole of the members early on Sunday mornings are – I regret to admit – the most (and perhaps only) reprehensible part of our creed. Those written confessions are to my mind disgusting and repulsive in their detail. The secret sins of men, women, girls and boys are openly proclaimed, while in the case of the elder members the confessions are still more grossly immodest, and sometimes terrible!" '

On July 14, 1888, the *Chatham and Rochester Observer* published another interview with an ex-member of the sect. This person objected particularly to Queen Esther's alleged arbitrary rule and merciless treatment of people who opposed her will. According to this informant, Queen Esther had been a far greater bigot than Jezreel, and much more ignorant than he. Unlike him she did not know how to 'manage' people: and, in fact, she would hardly allow them to think for themselves. Because Mr. Coupe, the secretary of the sect, refused to dispose of some books which she considered superfluous, but which he valued, she made herself so objectionable to him that he resigned his office and left Gillingham.

' "Unless you bent your will to hers in every detail of life", the informant continued, "you could go at once without any ceremony. It was nothing to her that you had given up your home and come away from your friends. . . . That did not weigh one iota with her. It did not matter if you were a father, mother, or child. Out you went if you dared to cross her will!" '

The process of putting people 'out' was known in the sect as 'cutting-off'; and Queen Esther, cognizant perhaps of her propensity to impose this extreme penalty, and certainly remembering the awkward case of Noah Drew, took steps to ensure that no 'cut-off' member should pursue her afterwards with claims for repayment of monies contributed to the treasury. According to the informant of the *Chatham and Rochester News*, she summoned a meeting of the leading members of the sect, and of others who had given large sums to the treasury, and she persuaded them all to sign a document which said that they fully understood that if they were ever 'cut-off', they would have no financial claim on Queen Esther personally, nor upon the 'New and Latter House of Israel'.

Despite the spate of criticism of Queen Esther from members whom she had offended or 'cut-off', to most of the sect she remained a true 'Servant of Israel'; and to some, indeed, she appeared to rank even higher than Jezreel himself. Mrs. Fanny Ball, one of Queen Esther's most devoted friends and followers, who supervised the household at 'Woodlands' for her, wrote a letter to the *Chatham and Rochester News* in December 1887 in which she boldly declared:

'The mission of the late Mr. Jezreel was indeed to establish the woman (Mrs. Jezreel) in her lawful position; and for this purpose he was called, chosen and sent of God. . . . Whether they like it or no, it is nevertheless true that it is by and through this woman, chosen of God before the foundations of the earth were laid, He is working His strange work, and bringing to pass "His Duty, His Strange Act". Did not the Jews reject Jesus, though the Lord chose Him? Even so do now all the Gentile churches reject the Woman upon whom He is pleased to bestow His Spirit for the ingathering of Israel . . .'

The untimely death of Queen Esther did not shake the faith of Mrs. Fanny Ball and many others who may have hoped, in their inward hearts, that she would prove immune to the earthly fate which had taken her husband from his flock. They explained that both Jezreel and Esther had been sent as trumpeters to proclaim God's message. Though both the instruments had been removed, the sound of the trumpets was ever audible to those who had ears to hear. Israel's faith was in no wise shaken by Queen Esther's death. Her mission in the flesh had been completed; now the work must be continued, for it was the Lord's work. . . .

A special article in the *Messenger of Wisdom and Israel's Guide* on Saturday, July 14, 1888, sought to make the position clear:

'THE DECEASE OF MRS. JEZREEL

Far from there being consternation among the members of the House of Israel at the death of any member, whether Mrs. Jezreel or the smallest child in our midst, we know and teach that all those who are to form the incorruptible Bride must depart before the full redemption can come to the 144,000 who will not sleep, not see death.'

The unavoidable question arose, however, who was to carry on the message now that Queen Esther had departed? The problem of the succession had been quickly resolved after Jezreel's death by Queen Esther's personality and determination. There was nobody however after she had gone who had the character and capacity necessary to ensure another undisputed 'reign'. Consequently, trials and tribulations were soon to confront the 'New and Latter House of Israel', and the faith of the members was tested to the uttermost.

X

ISRAEL DIVIDED

I N an article on the death of Queen Esther, the *Illustrated London News* on July 14, 1888 irreverently concluded:

'It will be interesting to see whether, having lost both prophet and queen, Jezreel and Co. (Ltd.) will go on or not. As they are said to have £50,000 invested in "plant" (of various kinds) it is probable that some spiritual person will be found to carry on the business.'

A 'spiritual person' of a decidedly eccentric type, even by Israel's standards, did indeed try, in due course, to stake his claim to the departed Queen Esther's inheritance. This person was Daniel Milton of Wrenthorpe, near Wakefield, Yorkshire. Milton, whose early life had been spent in the United States, called himself variously, 'Judge Milton', 'Archbishop Milton', 'The Promised Shiloh', and 'The Sixth Trumpeter'. He claimed also, as the last title indicated, to be the only legitimate successor to John Wroe. The latter, he said, had prophesied that the Christian-Israelites would come to be divided into three groups, 'two against the one, and the one against the two'. Milton himself was contending against a faction at Ashton-under-Lyne; and so it was clear, he said, that the other faction foretold by the prophet Wroe was the group of Israelites in Gillingham. The 'Sixth Church of Divine Revelation' of which he, Milton, was overseer, was the 'Established Church of Christ', against which the gates of hell (the tongues of mankind) would not prevail. The two factious communities, at Ashton and Gillingham, should therefore make submission to him.

The Jezreelites in Gillingham repulsed Milton's claims scornfully; but at the same time they realized that the succession to the

97

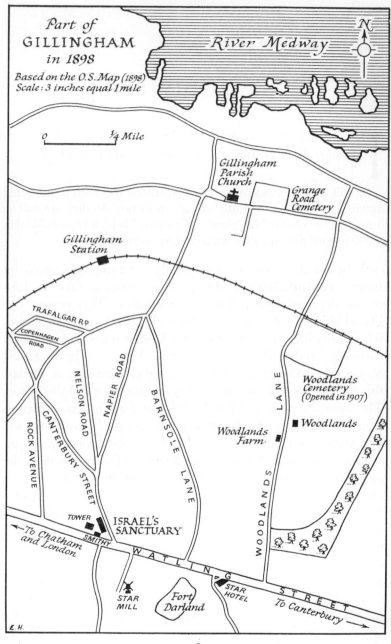

Part of
GILLINGHAM
in 1898

Based on the O.S. Map (1898)
Scale: 3 inches equal 1 mile

N

River Medway

0   ¼ Mile

Gillingham
Parish
Church

Grange
Road
Cemetery

Gillingham
Station

TRAFALGAR Rᵈ

COPENHAGEN
ROAD

NELSON ROAD

NAPIER ROAD

BARNSOLE LANE

WOODLANDS LANE

Woodlands
Cemetery
(Opened in 1907)

■ Woodlands

Woodlands
Farm

ROCK AVENUE

CANTERBURY STREET

TOWER

SMITHY

ISRAEL'S
SANCTUARY

←To Chatham
and London

WATLING   STREET

STAR
MILL

Fort
Darland

STAR
HOTEL

To Canterbury →

E. H.

leadership of the sect must be settled without delay. There was much earnest discussion, and for a while it was thought possible that little David Rogers might be the divinely-appointed successor to the Mother of Israel. This boy was the son of Queen Esther's brother Joshua, who a few years previously had been sent out to New Zealand with his wife to propagate the faith. Young David however had been kept home at 'Woodlands' by his aunt, because, it seems, she intended to train him for the succession.

Her early death ruined the boy's chances, for other members of the Rogers family, ambitious on their own account, brushed him aside. The two chief contenders were Edward Rogers, Queen Esther's father, and Mrs. Ann Rogers, one of her aunts. Both of these had played prominent parts in the life of the Gillingham community for many years. Edward Rogers, indeed, had dared even on occasion to challenge the great J. J. Jezreel himself. At one meeting during the latter's lifetime, for example, Edward Rogers contradicted Jezreel on a point of some kind or another, and seemed so sure of the rightness of his case that, as a member of the sect who was present declared, 'it was a question whether the Spirit was upon him or Jezreel!' The 'Messenger' had the courage and confidence to submit the issue to the vote of the members, and the dispute was settled in his favour.

Edward Rogers continued to play an important part in the affairs of the sect; and when his daughter died in 1888, and young David was rejected, only one other person had sufficient self-confidence to challenge his own bid for the leadership. This person was Ann, the wife of his brother John; and her challenge was strong, because she had the support of one or two influential members, such as John Maxwell, the schoolmaster of Israel's International College.

At last the struggle between Edward and Ann came to a climax, as a result of which it was decided that Edward should act as 'steward' or 'overseer' of the 'New and Latter House of Israel', presumably pending the arrival of a new divinely-inspired 'messenger' or 'trumpeter'. This compromise arrangement soon palled on Ann, and she broke away from Edward's stewardship, taking with her a good number of supporters, with whom she established a separate community in London, which claimed to be the lawful 'remnant'.

About this time, too, other small groups which refused to recognize the new regime under Edward Rogers broke away under leaders of their own. One such little body, called 'The Outcasts of Israel', was led by William Forsyth. He had learnt the faith in America, and after the death of Queen Esther he came to England and proclaimed that he alone had the key with which the mysteries of the *Flying Roll* could be unlocked. Forsyth's following came mostly from Jezreelites and others in the north of England; but in the south, mostly in London, another group formed themselves into a 'House of Israel and Jacob', while yet another, with headquarters at Harrow, styled themselves the 'House of Israel and Judah'.

Meanwhile, those (including Mrs. Emma Cave and other stalwarts) who had accepted Edward Rogers as overseer struggled on at Gillingham. On Saturday, July 14, 1888 the *Messenger of Wisdom* appeared as usual, but the first page stated, ambiguously, that the periodical was now 'Edited by Jezreel'. The editorial was headed 'Shiloh: The Leader of the House of Israel', and stated:

'The death during the past month of Mrs. Esther Jezreel, the editress of this paper, it is our painful duty to record. . . . That her mission was of God we, the House of Israel, know full well. What others may think and say we care not. Instead of being lowered, the Standard of Israel is floating higher today than ever. . . .'

Soon a rival of the *Messenger of Wisdom* appeared. This was a penny publication calling itself, challengingly, The *Pioneer of Wisdom*, and claiming to be 'A weekly newspaper devoted to the ingathering and restoration of Israel'. The proud editress of this new organ of the Press was Mrs. Ann Rogers, and in No. 1, which appeared on Friday, January 4, 1889, she wrote:

'The present visitation to Israel has extended over nearly a century, and during that time several instruments have been chosen of God to leave on record the revealed plan of a great and mighty work which the Lord will in these last days perform in His people Israel. . . . The sixth instrument in this visitation, who was the interpreter of the writings of the former messengers, before his death in 1885 oftimes expressed himself as anxious to have this weekly paper started. . . . We expect much opposition through our determination to hand forth the unalloyed teaching of Scripture.'

The calculated snub which the editress delivered to her brother-in-law Edward Rogers by omitting to mention that the *Messenger of Wisdom* had been started a year or two previously in compliance with Jezreel's wish, provoked the opposition from the rival camp which she had foreseen. The next and each succeeding issue of the *Messenger of Wisdom* bore a notice printed in bold type, headed IMPORTANT. It ran as follows:

'We wish our readers to particularly observe that a weekly paper styled *The Pioneer of Wisdom*, first issued on Friday, January 4, 1889, as coming from the New and Latter House of Israel, and purporting to be in conjunction with the *Messenger of Wisdom*, has no connection with either; neither have we given authority to those issuing it to advertise *Extracts from the Flying Roll* for sale. We simply warn our readers against those who by so doing are fraudulently usurping our rights, and thus laying themselves open to an action at law for damages.'

Mrs. Ann Rogers' rival pretensions, annoying though they were, proved of little consequence compared with the financial disaster which overtook the Gillingham group of believers shortly after Edward Rogers became overseer. After Messrs. Naylar had constructed the ground floor of the sanctuary, which housed the printing presses, Queen Esther commissioned them to complete the building, on the basis that as the work proceeded regular instalments of the money due would be paid by the Jez-reelites. At the time of Queen Esther's death operations had however already been suspended for three months, because the last instalment of money due to the builders, payable in March 1888, had not been paid. By that time about £30,000 had been spent on the building, and it was estimated that another £20,000 would be required to finish it.

By March 1888 the outer walls had been built up to the stipulated height, but unfortunately the roof had not been put on when
work was stopped. Thus the huge structure, surrounded by a
mass of scaffolding, lay completely at the mercy of wind and
rain. A notice was put up stating that 'Trespassers will be prosecuted', and to prevent defiance of the order the lower doors and
windows of the tower were blocked with large slabs of stone and
baulks of timber. Nevertheless, many inquisitive persons managed somehow to squeeze their way into the deserted interior:
and what an amazing sight met their eyes!

Scaffolding rose on every side; and the immense iron girders
designed to support the circular galleries or balconies of the
meeting hall, rising in tiers, made the interior of the tower look
like some immense, deserted circus ring. But over all brooded
the silence of inactivity. . . .

In this desperate situation Queen Esther, during the last few
months of her life, had had recourse to desperate remedies. She
tried to get various insurance companies to advance a loan to
enable building operations to be continued, but their surveyors
reported that the price which the property would fetch, if it had
to be sold to cover a mortgage, would be far less than the loan
required. The loan therefore was not forthcoming, and other
means of raising money to pay the builders not being available,
Messrs. Naylar obtained a court order which gave them possession of the property. As an interim arrangement, they agreed to
allow Edward Rogers and his followers to continue to use the
ground floor of the tower, containing the printing presses, and
the other buildings fronting Canterbury Street, on payment of
a small rent.

No sooner had one problem been settled, however, than another arose. On March 16, 1890, Noah Drew, the old defector
who had caused such trouble to Queen Esther, died after an
attack of bronchitis, at the age of seventy-four. Noah had been a
great favourite with the local inhabitants because of the courage
with which he had resisted the attempts of the Jezreelites to evict
him from his dwelling in Gillingham High Street. People were

The Tower as it looked when further work on it was stopped.

sorry for him, too, because he had lost all the money which he had contributed to the treasury, and had been reduced to a penurious old age.

Now that Noah had died, the local Press lost no time in raking over the embers of past controversies; and the shattered remnant of Israel, in addition to all its other troubles, soon found itself once again the centre of much unpleasant publicity. The *Chatham and Rochester Observer* chronicled Drew's death under the following headlines:

'DEATH OF A JEZREELITE
HOW NOAH DREW WAS TREATED
The old man gave all he possessed,
And then was nearly starved.'

Commenting, the paper once more attacked the sect very harshly:

'One of the most prominent supporters of the New and Latter House of Israel at the time the sect was first started, has just been removed from our midst by the hand of death. The tall and venerable-looking figure of Noah Drew was well known in New Brompton, and all who knew the history of his life and his surroundings during the last few years could not but feel sorry for the poor old man, whose appearance of late betokened no small amount of suffering and anxiety. And well might this be so, considering what he has had to pass through from the day when, unfortunately for himself and his family, the fatal spell of the doctrines (the term can only be used out of courtesy, for surely more unmitigated trash and heresy was never penned) cast its glamour over him. The history of Noah Drew may well serve as a warning to others. . . .'

The *Observer* reported that for the past three years Drew and his wife had been existing on a scanty diet of flour, bread and potatoes allowed them by the Jezreelites, who also provided them with firing for their single room in Mill Road. The *Observer* asserted that had it not been for the kindness of a few friends and neighbours, and a little money arriving from the United States from time to time, sent by Drew's sons, the old couple would have starved.

The Drews' situation must indeed have been parlous, for when Noah died Mrs. Drew was unable to provide for a 'respectable' burial, according to the standards of the time. She sent a friend, a Mr. Gowar, to call on Edward Rogers, therefore, requesting him to undertake this last duty on behalf of the sect. Edward Rogers however flatly refused to do anything at all, and justified his refusal by pointing out that Noah Drew was no longer a member, and had left of his own free will, moreover. Gowar replied that since the Jezreelites had had all Noah Drew's money, the least they could do in return would be to see that he had a decent burial. Edward Rogers flared up at this, and angrily told Gowar that since he himself professed to be such a close friend of Drew, the least *he* could do would be to bury him. Gowar, he added, had been 'the greatest thorn in the side of God's church'; and he predicted darkly that he would have to suffer for this by and by. To this Gowar answered that if having tried to prevent an old man from starving to death was sinning, then indeed he had sinned. ... Here Edward Rogers interrupted furiously, and warned Gowar to be careful of what he said about starvation.

Gowar was not intimidated, and replied that Noah Drew would have died years ago had it not been for the help of kind neighbours and friends. Now that he had died, however, if the Jezreelites would not see to his burial, the parish would have to do it. Edward Rogers nodded his head approvingly. Yes, he said, they were the proper authorities to carry out the funeral – and on this quite unrepentant note he ended the interview with the indignant Mr. Gowar.

For some reason or other the friends and neighbours who had succoured Noah Drew in the past did not now come forward to save him from the last indignity – a parish burial. Mrs. Drew had to apply to the Relieving Officer, and on Thursday afternoon, March 20, 1890, Noah Drew was lowered into a pauper's grave.

Edward Rogers' refusal to accept responsibility for the burial of Drew must have been caused as much by financial embarrassment as by any feelings of animosity. Since Esther's death and the defections of Ann Rogers and other members the sect's

income had seriously declined: and it was particularly unfortunate that several of the wealthier brethren, like Mr. Sliman, a
prosperous Mancunian, refused to acknowledge Edward Rogers
as overseer. Soon the position was so grave that Edward Rogers
had to relinquish, prematurely, the lease of 'Woodlands' which
he had taken out in March 1890 on the expiration of the previous
agreement.

With his faithful followers he moved to the row of buildings
adjacent to the sanctuary, and facing the top end of Canterbury
Street; and here they continued to run a dairy, a smithy, a bakery
and a laundry and, of course, the printing works situated on the
ground floor of the tower. For a time the Sunday evening services
open to the public were also held, but the chief attraction,
Israel's Band, had by now shrunk to a harmonium, three harps
and six violins, so the congregations grew smaller and smaller.

Although the sect had now declined to insignificance, the local
Press continued to pursue the remaining members venomously,
and a series of articles published in the *Chatham and Rochester
Observer* in September 1892 exceeded in vituperation any that had
previously appeared. The first article was published on September
17, 1892, under the heading:

'JEZREELISM EXPOSED
*Deceit, Oppression, and Spying.
Jezreel's Real Character.
Queen Esther's Jealousy.*'

The article began by stating that in the hope of obtaining some
as yet unpublished information a representative of the paper had
had an interview a few days previously with an ex-member of the
sect. The representative assured the readers of the paper that
every statement he now made could be 'authenticated even to the
minutest detail'.

The informant, who 'for various reasons' as usual wished to
remain anonymous, had formerly possessed a lucrative business
in one of the chief cities of Scotland. He became acquainted with
Jezreel, however, and like many others had been persuaded to

convert all his possessions into cash, which he donated to the 'Lord's Treasury' at 'Woodlands'. His later disenchantment caused him to revise his opinion of the 'Messenger', whom he described to the reporter as 'a deceitful man of the most wily type'. He claimed that he had spoken to officers of the 16th Foot, under whom Jezreel had served as a private soldier. The officers, he said, had told him that Jezreel had frequently overstayed his leaves, and had frequently had to be taken back to barracks in a drunk and disorderly condition.

After Jezreel's discharge from the army, the informant continued, he had carried on with his drinking habits at 'Woodlands', and to cover up these bouts after they had occurred, Queen Esther used to excuse his wild appearance by telling members that he had just come out of a trance, in which he had been seeing visions. The informant added that he, personally, was quite convinced that Jezreel's drinking habits had brought about his early death.

The ex-member was equally scathing about the way in which the sect had been financed in its palmy days.

' "There was, and still is," he said, "a system of robbery which goes by the name of tithe, under which so much has to part to the church. Where however a member had any property, he or she was urged to turn it into cash, and to gather at the headquarters, where all would share alike – but as a matter of fact they did not share alike. Jezreel and the Rogers family had the best of everything, while those who had provided the money had to put up with cabbages, peas, beans etc. and all sorts of oppression . . . more especially if they evinced the least sign of discontent at the treatment they received." '

Under Queen Esther the regime had become 'ten thousand times worse than before', according to the informant.

' "The food supply," he went on, "small as it was before, began to go down, and in consequence we were compelled to become almost vegetarians. She also extended the spying system, until there was no peace or safety anywhere, and life became nearly intolerable. Everybody was watched, and this was the foundation of three-fourths of the misery which prevailed in the church." '

In his concluding remarks, directed against Queen Esther, the informant declared that she had been excessively jealous; and after Jezreel's death had tried hard to discover, by means of the confessional system practised in the private services, whether her husband had been unfaithful to her. The informant was honest enough to add that no such evidence had been produced: and, he said, speaking for himself, he absolved Jezreel absolutely from any suspicions of immorality whilst he had been head of the church.

Triumphantly dotting the i's and crossing the t's of the special article, the editorial in the same issue of the *Chatham and Rochester Observer* remarked:

'The Jezreelite cult has been pretty well exposed by this time, but the further facts as to the lives and methods of certain of the leaders of that organization, which we have published in our last and present issues, must convince any remnant of the deluded people that they have been victims of designing rogues. With a pretence of sanctity and an assumption of religious mystery, these self-designated "Princes" have led lives of outrageous coarseness and immorality, and have enjoyed themselves at the expense of credulous mystics, who fancied that they had gained admission to a select circle of "the elect", and to the inner mysteries of the Universe.'

The reaction of Edward Rogers and his followers to all this abuse was silence – or, if they did write letters of rebuttal to the Press, the letters were never published. Meanwhile, the position of the faithful went from bad to worse. In July 1905, the owners of the property decided not to renew the lease under which Edward Rogers and his followers had occupied the ground floor of the tower, and the buildings in Canterbury Street. The decision was probably due to the fact that the rent was in arrears, and the Jezreelites could therefore no longer be counted upon to pay it regularly in future.

The trustees of Mr. Naylar the builder had sold the property to three partners, Messrs. Bowdage, Pedley and Tanton, and these, on July 17, 1905 entered into an agreement with Benjamin Cooper, a local builder, that he should demolish the tower down to the second floor joists. Cooper undertook in return to pay the partners £320, and they further agreed that he should be allowed to sell for his own profit all brickwork and other material resulting from the demolition, which was to be completed by April 28, 1906.

Edward Rogers and his followers were still in possession of the premises, and, moreover, owed a quarter's rent. The partners first tried to get this money, and on Friday, July 28 they sent a broker to Edward Rogers to demand the rent. After a short argument Rogers paid this, hoping no doubt to secure thereby an extension of the lease from the landlords. He was soon grievously disabused. Shortly after noon on the very same day a demolition foreman entered the sanctuary, followed by a gang of tough-looking navvies, who forthwith climbed to the top of the tower and began pulling down the brickwork with gusto.

The noise of the clanging hammers and the fall of the debris attracted the attention of the Jezreelites, who dashed out from their shops, led by Edward Rogers. The women began to weep when they saw what was happening, while the men stood glaring sullenly but impotently at the figures wrecking the top of the tower. Quickly, as the news of the demolition spread, a crowd of curious onlookers gathered to watch events.

They hoped for some excitement, and they were not disappointed. The Jezreelites maintained a small herd of dairy cows to supply the shop which they ran in the Canterbury Street premises, and the cows, which grazed a neighbouring pasture, were brought into the grounds adjoining the tower each afternoon to be milked. This day, however, the Jezreelite leading the beasts back to their milking-place found his entry into the grounds barred by a gatekeeper newly installed by the owners. This insult was too much for the long-suffering Edward Rogers. Calling on his male followers, about a dozen in all, he dashed towards the closed gate, and a sharp struggle took place during which the Jezreelites managed to tear the gate down. Before the cows could be let through, however, reinforcements arrived to help the gateman. These were the navvies, who soon routed the Jezreelites, and placed the gate triumphantly in position again. The *Daily*

Chronicle of July 30, reporting this brief but spirited encounter, commented:

'The old leader fought like a lion, and pummelled a gigantic navvy manfully, although his opponent, strong enough to kill him, took it all good-naturedly, and only pushed the infuriated old man out of the gate.'

Refusing to accept defeat, Edward Rogers sent for the police, and pending their arrival he maintained a wordy warfare with the navvies and their foremen, while the poor cows looked on disconsolately. When the police arrived from Chatham and the situation was explained to them, they had no alternative but to give the decision in favour of the navvies. And so Edward Rogers and his followers had to make yet another move in their sad pilgrimage. They managed to get accommodation in Cleveland Villa, a detached house at the top end of Napier Road, and in several other houses in the neighbourhood of the tower; and now out of sorrow a measure of comfort came, for many 'Gentiles' called on the Jezreelites at their new addresses to assure them of their sympathy.

A representative of the *Chatham and Rochester News* who called at Cleveland Villa in August 1905 to find out what the future plans of the group were was told that no immediate resumption of the public services could be expected. When he asked about rumours that Israel's International College had closed down the answer came pat that it had: but, the spokesman of the sect told the reporter, only because 'all the children have now grown up'.

The *Messenger of Wisdom*, too, had come to a sudden end on July 30, 1905, because the demolition men had taken over the tower, on the ground floor of which it was printed. As a culminating indignity, the sanctuary, in view of its approaching demolition, was advertised in the local Press as a kind of gigantic peep-show. An advertisement appeared in the *Chatham and Rochester News* on August 5, 1905, which stated:

'LAST OF THE JEZREEL TOWER
Visitors will be admitted to the Jezreel Tower on Sunday and Monday.

The contractors' men will be in attendance.

This will be the last opportunity of inspecting this extraordinary and unique building!'

In fact, the 'last opportunity' of viewing the tower was not to come until many years later. The building proved remarkably stubborn in its resistance to the demolition men; and the faith, too, though at so low an ebb, refused to die. Soon the most extraordinary of all the so-called 'Messengers' came to stake his claim in Gillingham in an attempt to revive the flagging fortunes of the 'New and Latter House of Israel'. He was rejected with contumely by Edward Rogers and the faithful handful of followers who remained; but the words and deeds of the new pretender, savouring of tragi-comedy, were to keep the Jezreelites, and the tower, intermittently in the news until after the First World War.

XI

PRINCE MICHAEL AND THE
NEW EVE

A MONG the vexations suffered by Edward Rogers and his followers after Queen Esther's death was a visit by an importunate American who called himself 'Prince Michael', and claimed to be the next 'Messenger' or 'Trumpeter' in succession to Jezreel.

The real name of the visitor was Michael Keyfor Mills, and he had been born in Detroit in 1857. His father had died when Michael was only six years old, so the boy was sent to Canada to be brought up in the home of his grandfather, the Reverend Thomas Mills, a Baptist minister. Here young Michael showed a precocious interest in, and aptitude for, engines of all kinds, and so he was trained as a mechanic. At the age of eighteen he was a foreman in a hammer factory, and he later acquired some valuable engineering experience in Canada. When he was twenty-five he started a small factory of his own, and when, shortly afterwards, he married, he seemed set for the normal uneventful career of the prosperous businessman.

But it was not to be. One evening in the year 1888 when he returned home his wife, Rosetta, excitedly told him that a woman had called with a book called the *Flying Roll*. The book proved, by many biblical references, that some chosen people would never die. . . .

This story interested Mills greatly, for during his upbringing at his grandfather's house he had acquired a keen interest in the Bible, and this he never lost. When therefore his wife suggested that the woman, Miss Eliza Court, whose address she had taken, should be invited to call again, Mills readily agreed.

When the lady reappeared, he plied her with many earnest

III

questions, all of which, by reference to the *Flying Roll*, she answered to his complete satisfaction. He bought a copy from her and studied it very carefully; and it so convinced him of the truth of Jezreel's message that he became a fervent member of the 'New and Latter House of Israel'. He let his hair and beard grow, and came to spend more and more of his time distributing copies of the *Flying Roll* (which he paid for out of his own pocket) to persons who, prayer had revealed to him, were likely to benefit from a perusal of its doctrines. Gradually he came to believe that he was specially chosen by God to expound the doctrines. Heavenly voices spoke to him and told him to go forth preaching; so he disposed of his business, and with his wife and Eliza Court he travelled around the state of Michigan, selling copies of the *Flying Roll*, and endeavouring to win converts to the 'New and Latter House of Israel'.

In 1891 came a call, in most mysterious fashion, to assume the leadership left vacant by the death of Queen Esther three years previously. One day he suddenly asked his wife to anoint his head with oil, and shortly after she had obligingly done this, she cried out:

'The yoke of evil shall be broken because of the anointed!'

Mills replied 'Thank God!', and immediately he had uttered this cryptic remark his hands were jerked up into the air by supernatural force, and rubbed against each other with a swift movement entirely beyond his control. Next, the same invisible power raised him from the ground, and with his right arm stretched towards heaven, he cried aloud in a strange voice:

'Prince Michael has come! Prince Michael has come!'

It was, at last, his call!

Basing his claims on certain passages in the *Flying Roll*, which he had certainly studied to good effect, he now declared that he was the 'Prince Michael' referred to in the Book of Daniel:

'I will shew thee that which is noted in the scripture of truth; and there is none that holdeth with me in these things, but Michael your prince.' (x, 21.)

'And at that time shall Michael stand up, the great prince which standeth for the children of thy people; and there shall be a time of trouble, such as never was since there was a nation even to that same time: and at that time thy people shall be delivered, every one that shall be found written in the book.' (xii, 1.)

Michael soon had about one hundred and fifty credulous followers, who met in a so-called 'God-house' on the outskirts of Detroit, and this initial success encouraged him to make a trip to Gillingham to try to get his claim accepted there. He was received by Edward Rogers at 'Woodlands' in January 1892, and at once tried to win over the 'overseer' by promises that if the sect took him as the new 'Messenger' he would complete the sanctuary, and in other ways restore Israel's declining fortunes. Edward Rogers and the other Jezreelites would have nothing to do with Michael, however; and so the discomfited 'Prince' returned to Detroit.

Here a scandal of the first magnitude soon overtook him. He was arrested on a charge of seducing a young girl named Bernice Bechel, aged fifteen, whom he had placed in the 'God-House' with her parents' consent, ostensibly to help with the services. Information about much more profane rites soon came to the ears of Mills' wife, Rosetta, who already suspected that her husband's relationship with Eliza Court was not kept on an exclusively spiritual plane. Rosetta brought an action for divorce, alleging adultery and immorality, and so the alleged seduction of Bernice Bechel came to light, and Prince Michael was charged with a criminal offence against the girl.

At the trial the jury took only fifteen minutes before returning a verdict of guilty, and Prince Michael was given the maximum sentence – imprisonment for five years. He was released in 1896, after having served four years, and on his release at once resumed his religious activities in the 'God-House', not one whit abashed by his experience. He was received with joy by Eliza Court, whom he now married and accorded the title of 'Princess Michael'. She and many of his followers believed that he was quite innocent of the charge which had been preferred against him. They considered, indeed, that he had been 'framed' by the police, and had borne his martyrdom in noble fashion. Supported thus by the faithful, Prince and Princess Michael carried on quietly and unobtrusively at Detroit till, in 1905, news of the disastrous events at Gillingham – the departure of Edward Rogers and his followers from 'Woodlands' and their subsequent eviction from the sanctuary – tempted Prince Michael to try his fortune in England once again.

He arrived on April 5, 1906, accompanied by Princess Michael, his secretary Mr. Mackay, and a small band of his Detroit followers, among whom was the organist, appropriately named Brother Wroe Harmony. At once the local Press, which for months had been starved of sensational titbits concerning the Jezreelites, scented a 'story'. Reporters were dispatched posthaste to interview the newcomer and his retinue, to ascertain their plans.

Michael, his red, pitted face beaming benevolently, was very willing to oblige. Dressed in a brown suit of ample proportions, and wearing a broadbrimmed hat of transatlantic style, he looked like a backwoodsman of the Wild West come to town. A slightly incongruous touch was added by his long grey beard which reached over his protuberant stomach, partly concealing a heavy gold watchchain which seemed to suggest that Michael, at least, had found propagation of the faith a profitable business recently. He genially answered a few questions put to him by the reporter of the *Chatham and Rochester Observer*, but then apparently tiring, and exclaiming whimsically 'I don't want to blow my own horn!' he referred the reporter to his private secretary, Mr. Mackay.

Mackay in some respects was an even more curious person than his chief. His parents had given him the Christian names David Livingstone as a tribute to the explorer and missionary, for Mackay's father was a well-known Presbyterian minister. Young Mackay himself had originally trained for the church at Edinburgh University, but having come across a copy of the *Flying Roll* one day he read it, and, so he said, found 'grace and truth' in it. He paid a visit to the headquarters of the sect at Gillingham, but he took a dislike to Edward Rogers, and so went to on London to see whether he could accept the leadership of Mrs. Ann Rogers. She pleased him no more, and he was like a lost sheep until he heard one day of the 'God-house' in Detroit. So he journeyed thither, still in search of the true leader of Israel, and as soon as he saw Prince Michael he knew, as he declared later, that he was 'right home'. From then onwards he was always at Prince Michael's side, and became one of his most devoted – and curious – followers.

Physically Mackay was a handsome and imposing man, which made the tragedy of his extravagances all the more sad. His pale oval face, and his long hair and beard gave him a striking resemblance to the traditional portraits of Christ; and his manner, and speech too, were of an educated man. If appearances were anything to go by, Prince Michael could have had no better henchman. Alas, the mind that functioned within the imposing exterior was of a kind that swiftly shattered any impression of normality which might have been formed by anybody seeing Mackay for the first time.

Replying to the *Chatham and Rochester Observer* reporter's questions, Mackay explained at length why Prince Michael had decided to come to Gillingham. Primarily, it was in fulfilment of the prophecy in the Book of Daniel xii, 1, and the mission of Michael was to complete the work begun by Jezreel. Under Edward Rogers that work had suffered grievously. The members had been scattered, the sanctuary despoiled. All this had happened because Edward Rogers had not been appointed by God. In 1891 Prince Michael had travelled all the way from Detroit to Gillingham to inform Edward Rogers and the Jezreelites that the Holy Spirit had selected him to be the next 'Messenger' to complete the 'work'. Prince Michael had been rebuffed; but he had returned to Detroit undismayed, knowing full well that God, in His own good time, would fully vindicate the rights of His new 'Messenger'.

Meanwhile, Mackay continued, clear proof had been given that Prince Michael had been visited by the Holy Spirit, for he had

115

demonstrated on many occasions that he had the gift of healing. To quote only a small instance, the Prince had only to lay his hand on Mackay's head, and Mackay's headaches disappeared at once. More than this, however, the Prince had the gift of prophecy. As the ship which bore him to England left harbour, the Spirit moved Michael to raise his arm and declaim: 'Woe! Woe! Woe! to this land of the West!' Shortly afterwards a terrible earthquake wrecked San Francisco, and Michigan was ravaged by widespread fires. Now, said Mackay significantly, both San Francisco and Michigan had reviled Prince Michael and his followers. . . .

The reporter now ventured to touch on a very delicate subject, and asked Mackay for his version of Prince Michael's trial and prison sentence. Mackay at once affirmed that the entire business had been a gross miscarriage of justice. The police had raided the 'God-House', and a number of women and girls – wives, sisters and daughters of members – had been arrested and kept in custody for three months, amongst them Mackay's own wife. During this period they had been subjected to third-degree methods, and some of the young girls had succumbed to this mental torture, and had signed confessions which led to Prince Michael's arrest, trial and imprisonment. The Prince, however, was completely innocent of the charge against him, and the girls later bitterly repented the physical frailty which had led them to give false witness. Indeed, they would willingly have gone to gaol themselves to save him, if they could have done. But, said Mackay gravely, that could not be permitted, for it would have interfered with the fulfilment of the prophecy 'Out of prison he comes to reign.'

Prince Michael, taking inspiration from Volume I of the *Extracts from the Flying Roll*, had decided to rename the church 'The New Eve, or New House of Israel', but he meant strictly to carry on and complete Jezreel's work. He had come to Gillingham to put an end to the disastrous regime of Edward Rogers; and Israel's Sanctuary, which would be renovated and completed, would henceforth be known as 'Mount Zion'. Israel's

International College would be refounded, and would soon be crowded with students from all parts of the world intent on studying the *Flying Roll*. Finally, of course, in the great consummation of the work, the 144,000 would be gathered in at Gillingham at the end of the last watch. When the reporter, trying to get a word in edgeways, interrupted Mackay at length to ask how all Prince Michael's ambitious projects were to be financed, the answer came at once, delivered with complete confidence and touching faith: the money would be provided in the fullness of time by God.

Prince Michael tried hard once again to get Edward Rogers and the remnant of the Jezreelites living in Gillingham to accept him, but without success. The *Messenger of Wisdom* till its end continued to publish in each issue a notice which had first appeared after Prince Michael's initial visit to Gillingham. The notice read, ungrammatically:

'CAUTION

Michael Mills and Eliza Court of America having set up a church of their own there and are publishing a paper with a view of propagating their own ideas upon the *Flying Roll*, the public are cautioned that they are in no way connected with the House of Israel. We desire to draw attention to the fact that all such workings proceed from false brethren WITHIN the House of Israel, and all are referred to on the first page of the first sermon of the *Flying Roll*. Similar false teachers and deceitful workers who troubled Paul in his day are the only ones who could imitate the truth and work so closely as to deceive (if it were possible) the very elect.'

Undeterred by Edward Rogers' denunciations, Prince Michael and his little group of followers persevered with their plans, and as a first step towards the establishment of Mount Zion took a lease of the Jezreelite buildings at the top end of Canterbury Street. Letters were sent to members of the 'New and Latter House of Israel' in different parts of Britain and abroad, inviting them to join the 'New Eve' and assemble at Mount Zion.

Meanwhile, Prince Michael, profiting from his unfortunate brush with the Press in the United States, and bearing in mind the consequences which had flowed from Queen Esther's disregard of public opinion in England, set out to win over the local newspapers to his side. On June 2, 1906 the following letter, addressed to the editor, appeared in the *Chatham and Rochester Observer*:

> 'Mount Zion,
> New Brompton,
> May 29, 1906.

Dear Sir,

Prince Michael wishes me to convey his thanks for the kind and courteous consideration which you have given to the cause to which he has, by the direction of God, devoted his life.

Yourself, or representative, will always receive the same courtesy in return; and be assured that any communications which are of interest to the public will be cheerfully given from time to time as the new movement develops.

> I am, dear sir,
> Yours faithfully,
> David Livingstone Mackay,
> (Private Secretary to Prince Michael).'

Having established himself with the editor, Mackay was able to get the *Chatham and Rochester Observer* on June 9, 1906, to publish in full a most curious correspondence which he had latterly carried on with the recalcitrant Edward Rogers. The exchange illustrates the stage of tragi-comedy to which Michael and Mackay were now reducing the fortunes of Israel. Mackay opened with a letter to Rogers dated from 'Mount Zion, 551 Canterbury Road, May 28, 1906'. The letter began in regal style, but continued with scant regard for grammar:

'To Edward Rogers, Greeting!

Michael, your Prince, wishes to give an opportunity to yourself and all interested in the *Flying Roll* to come forward and lend their support in the rebuilding of the Sanctuary.

It greatly grieves your Prince to see the dismal state in which the Remnant of the former House and the Sanctuary itself now lies in, but with God's help he believes all can be restored and the new House be made to exceed in glory that of the former under the leadership of James Jezreel.

Michael is desirous to be found standing with the Lord's chosen messengers James and Esther Jezreel, and in obedience to the Word revealed in the *Flying Roll*. . . .'

After quoting copiously from the *Flying Roll* to prove that Prince Michael was the lawful successor of James and Esther Jezreel, Mackay went on:

'If Eliza Court, now Princess Michael, is not that woman foretold by Jezreel as "The New Eve" and "Princess of Life" who was then in the House, and Michael Mills, now Prince Michael, not that man whose name is "The Branch" who shall build the temple of the Lord according to the words of the prophet Zechariah (vi, 12), where are they, and who are they?

Did not Jezreel faithfully warn you not to do to the "seventh" as the John Wroe House did to him, and also to beware lest you became the "Old House"? But you heeded not the warning, and the thing has come upon you.

Now, according to the Chronicles of Israel, the month of May is to decide the final destiny of Man, wherefore we exhort you to weigh well what is herein written, that it may be well with you and all who desire to know and do the will of God.

I am,
LITTLE DAVID, as of old.'

To this strange missive Edward Rogers replied as follows:

'360 Canterbury Street,
Date: Last day of the fatal month in
the destiny of Man.
To: Mr. David Mackay, alias "David of old".
Dear Brother,

After a prolonged search through both Bible and *Roll* I have come to the conclusion that there is no advantage to be gained either financially or otherwise in assuming to be one who lived and died centuries ago.

In hope of you seeing your error,
A Believer in the Teaching of the Word
that "Names stand for Nothing'.*

* Quoted from the writings of J. J. Jezreel, in whom you profess to believe.'

119

In reply to these gentle chidings 'Little David' returned to the attack in a long reply dated June 1, which ended thus:

'Methinks Little David has not only administered the "five smooth stones" from the Brook of Truth upon thy brow, but also turned back thine own words upon thee, and taken off thy head, which is the work my Father has commissioned me to do in this spiritual warfare and great Battle of the Ages (Revelation, vii, 7) – "Michael and his angels fought against the dragon" – for the possession of the Temple (the body of man in immortality).

I am,

DAVID THE "LIVING STONE",
Slayer of Goliath,
Lieutenant of Prince Michael.'

Mackay also from time to time enriched the pages of the local Press with letters containing dire warnings that death would infallibly overtake all those who refused to subscribe to the teachings of the *Flying Roll*, as interpreted, of course, by Prince Michael. He was forever telling people of the disastrous consequences of opposing the Prince; and he never hesitated to quote some awful examples as a warning.

The San Francisco earthquake and the Michigan forest fires were, of course, favourite themes; but Mackay was also fond of quoting what had happened to the Canadian postal authorities, and Lord and Lady Minto, for refusing to comply with the Prince's wishes. The postal authorities had sinned because they declined to allow the *Flying Roll* to be sent through the post. Retribution overtook them shortly afterwards, said Mackay, when the Ottawa Post Office was burnt to the ground. As for Lord and Lady Minto, when Mackay had written to Lord Minto, the Governor-General of Canada, asking him to annul the ruling of the postal authorities, he, Mackay, had received no answer. Consequently, retribution fell on Lord Minto and his wife. While skating on the Toronto Ice Rink Lady Minto fell and broke her leg; and Rideau Hall, the official residence of the Governor-General, was, like the Ottawa Post Office, burned down to the ground.

Despite the extravagant behaviour of Prince Michael and Mackay, and their nonsensical pretensions, they did not lack followers, and funds were soon sufficient to enable the 'New Eve' to rent the tower and the outlying buildings on Canterbury Street. Here Prince Michael opened a general store and a refreshment room, and he also used another part of the premises as a lecture hall and a place for the public services which he conducted. By October 1909 however funds were beginning to run short, and Prince Michael was £50 in arrears with the rent. The owners of the property then obtained an eviction order, and on October 19 this was enforced by a sheriff's officer, accompanied by an assistant, and a police sergeant and constable. The Jezreelites on the premises in Canterbury Street refused to leave, and force had to be applied to eject the men, while the women stood mournfully by seeking consolation from the Bibles which they held in their hands. Whilst the eviction was taking place Prince Michael had been in the tower; but on learning about it he marched over to the scene of the conflict, accompanied by his wife and his private secretary. For a full hour he stood and argued with the sheriff's officer, whilst the police and a large crowd looked on. He alleged that the sheriff's officer and his accomplices were persecutors of the church, and he stated, boldly, that he recognized no instructions or orders from Man, but only those revealed to him as coming from God. It was all to no avail, however; and the most that he could achieve was an arrangement whereby, in recognition of the fact that he at last paid the £50 rent which he owed, his followers were allowed to retrieve from the buildings all their personal possessions. By four-thirty in the afternoon the last of them had departed, and Mount Zion was left in charge of a caretaker.

The eviction of Prince Michael and his followers from the 'Sanctuary' must have awakened unhappy memories in the mind of Edward Rogers; for only a few years previously he himself, and his own faithful band, had suffered the same indignity. Rogers made use of the misfortune of Prince Michael, however, to draw attention once again to the heretical nature of the 'New Eve'. A letter which was published in the *Chatham and Rochester News* on October 30, 1909, cautioned the public as follows:

'To the Editor.

The New and Latter House of Israel.
Re Jezreel's Tower.

Sir,

We wish it to be distinctly understood that we are in no way what-ever connected with Michael Keyfor Mills, styling himself 'Prince Michael', neither has he any connections with the New and Latter House of Israel, or any right whatever to use the name "Jezreel". . . . Furthermore, we are not, and will not be, responsible for any debts he or his followers may contract, either under his own name or the name of "Jezreel".

We publish this in no spirit of hostility, but simply to protect our rights.

Edward Rogers,
Trustee for the New and Latter House of Israel,
185, Nelson Road, New Brompton.'

The irrepressible Prince Michael was not in the least discon-certed by Edward Rogers' letter, nor by his eviction from Mount Zion. Following Edward Rogers' own example of a few years before, he rented some houses near the tower for himself and his followers, and waited a chance to reinstall them in the buildings fronting Canterbury Street, for he considered that occupation of at least part of the Sanctuary was essential to lend colour to his pretensions.

He managed, as a matter of fact, to return to the buildings as the result of a curious agreement which he made in 1912 with a Mr. Worrall, the Principal of the Gillingham School of Dancing, who had leased the upper part of the premises. Mr. Worrall used these rooms only during the winter months, when he held his dancing classes, and so he willingly agreed to sublet them to Prince Michael during the summer months. The Prince began to use the rooms for services, and to advertise these he plastered a glass-fronted door which gave access to the street with all kinds of strange notices. One of the most extraordinary of these referred to the recent disaster when the *Titanic* was sunk by an iceberg. Prince Michael's notice read:

'SS. TITANIC

By the sinking of the above vessel a special warning has been given and symbol shown of the coming fall of Babylon. In addition to the prophecies referred to above (in another notice) this fall was also fore-told by the late James Jershom Jezreel in the *Flying Roll* Series 3, page 222, which speaks of the horse and his rider (Christendom) being overthrown in the sea. In the sinking of the *Titanic* the prophecy has received its fulfilment in figure, the horse being symbolized by Mr. Stead, the "steed" of Christendom, and the rider by Mr. Astor. . . .[1] The boat was considered unsinkable, but she was swallowed up by the waters, and Babylon will just as certainly fall, for the one is the figure of the other.'

Prince Michael's sublease of the rooms was to end on August 31, 1912, and on that day Mr. Worrall and his wife came to pre-pare them for the resumption of the dancing classes. While Mrs. Worrall was upstairs cleaning the rooms out, Mr. Worrall began to remove Prince Michael's announcements and notices from the front door. While he was doing this the Prince appeared, accom-panied by six of his followers armed with sticks, and they all promptly set about the unfortunate dancing instructor. Prince Michael punched him on the jaw, and his followers belaboured Mr. Worrall with their sticks. The noise of the fracas caused Mrs. Worrall to poke her head outside the upstairs window, and her screams soon attracted a big crowd. The followers of Prince Michael had meanwhile locked and barricaded the door, so that Mrs. Worrall was a prisoner. Some brave spirits now went to fetch a ladder to rescue her, and recognizing that numbers were against them, Prince Michael and his six braves stealthily departed by means of the back door.

The Prince was later charged with assault by Mr. Worrall, and appeared at Chatham Police Court on September 9. He caused no little astonishment by coming dressed in a bright blue suit, set off by large brown boots: and the whole effect was made much

[1] W. T. Stead, famous English journalist and publicist, and Colonel John Jacob Astor, both passengers on the ship.

more striking by his long beard and moustaches, and his flowing locks, let down specially for the occasion. He pleaded not guilty, but the magistrates fined him forty shillings, with £1 15s. 6d. costs; and though he unwillingly paid up, he left court an aggrieved man, feeling that once again he had been the victim of a miscarriage of justice. Unrepentantly, he caused the following notice to be brought to the attention of the public:

'The Spiritual and Temporal Courts of Our God and of the New Eve Church justify Prince Michael according to the laws of God and the laws of the land in putting Mr. Worrall out of the building for tearing down and trampling underfoot the Word of God, and refusing to desist when requested.

The New Eve, the New House or Body of Israel,
September 9, 1912

One of the most extraordinary features of Prince Michael's chequered career was that whenever money was required for the purposes of the 'New Eve', he was able to provide it. A small part of his income was derived from a refreshment room and a general store which his followers, in accordance with Jezreelite tradition, ran in Gillingham. Most of his funds must, however, have come from contributions; and as the number of his followers in Britain was very small, he probably depended on remittances from across the Atlantic to keep himself solvent.

Whatever the source of his income, he was able in May 1914 to realize a long-cherished ambition, and take up residence in 'Woodlands', the house which was hallowed for all true Israelites because of its associations with Jezreel and Queen Esther. After Edward Rogers had been forced to leave 'Woodlands' the property came into the possession of Louis Brennan the inventor, of torpedo and monorail fame. Brennan left Gillingham for London however in September 1912, and Gillingham Town Council bought 'Woodlands' from him for £2,500, after it had been previously offered for auction but had failed to reach the reserve price put on it.

Prince Michael now began a long campaign with the object of getting the Council to lease the house to him on favourable terms

– or even, as he fondly hoped, to sell it to him at bargain price. The Council rejected his first applications, and then, to quote the *Chatham and Rochester News* of January 10, 1914, he sent a long letter to each individual member of the Council 'which could only be described as audaciously saucy'. The letter read:

'Sir,

We are in receipt of your favour of late date, informing us of the Council's decision that the "Woodlands" is not for rent or sale.

We have a fresh proposition to lay before the Council, which is that they give Prince Michael the use of the property free of cost or any charge whatever, which would do away with any discussion of rent or purchase. The simple fact that Prince and Princess Michael like the "Woodlands" and desire it for a residence, ought to be sufficient reason to at once grant the request without further argument.

That it is the Son of Man, the Ambassador of the Living God of Israel, a preacher in high favour with God, who now gives the "city fathers" such an opportunity of showing their favour and friendliness towards the only one who stands with God in those things which are noted in the Scripture of Truth (Daniel x, 21) is an honour and privilege which any man or body of men should be anxious to accept, who are not totally blind to their own best interests and the interests of the people they are appointed to represent. . . . Prince Michael is willing to throw open the large room at the "Woodlands" known as the billiard room to members of the Council at least one evening each week (*Note of editor:* "Here follows a parenthetical remark about the wives of the members of the Council – a remark which is in shockingly bad taste to say the least") and to explain to them his mission for the ingathering and restoration of Israel. . . .'

Prince Michael also referred to the associations 'spiritual and otherwise' of the house, which, he declared, made it desirable that he and his followers should live in it. Finally, in accordance with his invariable practice, the Prince warned the Council that terrible retribution would overtake them should they ignore his pleas, or treat him in any way harshly or unkindly.

Michael's very persistence seems to have had an effect, for in the end the Council agreed to lease 'Woodlands' to him. Various stipulations were made, however, one being that the property should be used only as a residence, though, in view of Prince Michael's pretensions, it was conceded that he might hold religious services there. The most important clause of the agreement from the Council's point of view, perhaps, was that the rent was to be paid in advance, with a first payment of £100 to be made before Prince Michael took up residence.

The money was duly paid; and in May 1914 Prince and Princess Michael and their retinue moved into the old home of Jezreel and Queen Esther. Here the Prince and his wife lived contentedly for the remaining years of their lives; and if the number of converts to the 'New Eve' did not grow perceptibly, at least the subscriptions from existing followers, and the income from the 'Jezreel' shops enabled the couple to live in modest comfort.

Plans for completing Israel's Sanctuary never ceased to run through his head, and he spent a great deal of his time showing people over the tower, and trying to coax money from them for the rebuilding fund. Meanwhile, always of a practical turn of mind, he converted the billiards room in 'Woodlands' into a private chapel, and here the services of the 'New Eve' were held with unfailing regularity.

In public Prince Michael became well-known in Gillingham, and well-liked. His predilection for startling-coloured clothes (a suit in the imperial purple was a particular favourite) invariably made him the centre of attention as he strode along the streets of the town, followed at a respectable distance by awestruck little boys. During these excursions, whenever he entered a shop to buy anything, his procedure was always the same. He would ask for a certain article, and on being told the price would silently ponder the matter over for a few moments. Then he would solemnly declare 'God has told me to buy this' or 'God has told me not to buy this', as the case might be.

The Prince was often to be seen in one of the first motor-cars, for he never lost his early aptitude for, and interest in, all things mechanical. His followers were as proud of this more earthly aspect of the Prince's character as they were of his spiritual qualifications, and one of them said once to a reporter:

126

'He is a thorough mechanic, and can make almost anything, from a pin to a steam-engine. He is a master of fifty trades!'

As a result of Prince Michael's passion for cars the lawns of 'Woodlands' were littered with spare parts, and vehicles in different stages of assembly or demolition, so that the place came to look more like an untidy rural garage than the headquarters of a religious group.

Even in his later years the Prince seemed fated to clash with authority. He had one or two more brushes with the law, and though fisticuffs were not involved as in his more robust days, the offences were serious enough to take him to court. On one occasion he declared that his religious principles forbade him to pay certain taxes; and when after a court order he remained obdurate, some of his furniture was taken from 'Woodlands' to pay for the arrears. On another occasion, in April 1920, Prince Michael had to appear before the Gillingham Profiteering Tribunal to answer an accusation that he had charged excessive prices for soda at his 'Jezreel' general stores in Napier Road. The charge was dismissed, and Prince Michael left the Mayor's Parlour, where the tribunal had been sitting, with an air of triumphant rectitude.

Death finally struck at him through his passion for cars. At the beginning of January 1922 he bought yet another second-hand model, and despite the prevailing cold weather he could not resist going for a trial run with Princess Michael. The effect of the journey on both proved fatal. They fell victims to the influenza epidemic which was raging at the time, and speedily succumbed. Princess Michael died first, on January 12, and the Prince followed her three days later, at the age of sixty-five.

A reporter of the *Chatham and Rochester Observer* paid a visit to the 'Woodlands' just before the funeral, and wrote:

'There was a very uncanny atmosphere about the place. The house presented a very forsaken appearance. There were no blinds or curtains to the windows, and inside lay piles of books and oddments of furniture, all in a curious mixture. Under the fir-trees at the front of the

127

house were beehives, and an assortment of stove-pipes and stoves, evidently placed there with a purpose.

On the lawn a large flock of fowls were clustering around pieces of bones and vegetables, and were not the least disconcerted by the number of old motor-cars in the vicinity. Only one of these cars seemed to be in a state of completion. The remainder were devoid of some principal portion, and had evidently been preserved by the Prince for experimental purposes. . . .'

Prince Michael and his faithful consort were buried together in the same grave, quietly and unostentatiously, in Woodlands Road Cemetery on Thursday morning, January 19, 1922.[1] There was little of the public interest which had been excited by the burial of Jezreel, and later of Queen Esther; and only a few curious onlookers attended, in addition to the members of the 'New Eve'. The burial service was dispensed with; but one last tribute had been paid to the deceased by their followers. Before the lids were screwed on to the coffins, three carnations had been placed by the side of Princess Michael, and three arum lilies on the breast of Prince Michael. This latter gesture was truly graceful, for it was meant to recall to the initiated that the Prince had always protested a great liking for those particular flowers, as symbols of purity.

Some comment was evoked after the funeral by the curious appearance of the hearse, one side window of which was shattered. It was disclosed by the undertaker's men that an accident had happened as Prince Michael's coffin was being placed inside, which led to the coffin smashing the window. To any connoisseur of the Prince's esoteric doctrines this curious happening must surely have seemed a sign of some sort from above; but his followers never stated whether they attached a supernatural significance to the mishap, or not. Though the interpretation therefore remains unsolved, it is at least pleasing to record that Prince Michael departed this life, as he would have wished, with one last, defiant gesture!

---

[1] The grave, No. 698, Class C, Section I, has a plain stone curb around it, but no memorial of any kind. Like the grave of Jezreel and Queen Esther in the neighbouring Grange Road Cemetery, it is in a sad state of neglect.

XII

ICHABOD, ICHABOD . . .

THE history of the Jezreelites after the First World War was one of steady decay, and by the time the second war began their numbers in Britain had so declined that the sect was on the point of extinction. The score or so of devotees who had followed Prince Michael were utterly dumbfounded by his death, and clung on at 'Woodlands' like lost sheep awaiting a new shepherd. One of them, a Miss Miller, was given permission to renew the tenancy of the house until May 1923, and when the extension expired the little community moved to Oxford. Here they lived for a few years, but in the end most of them returned to the United States.

The 'old guard' of the Jezreelites, led through so many vicis-situdes by their overseer Edward Rogers, father of Queen Esther, fared no better. The venerable old man died, and advancing years took a steady toll of his small group of followers, while no fresh converts were made. Up to the beginning of the Second World War one or two male Jezreelites, distinctive because of their long hair tucked up at the back of their heads, were still to be seen in the neighbourhood of the sanctuary, where they carried on small businesses or ran shops. Even they have now disappeared from the scene, and only a handful of members of the sect, very old persons, remain living in retirement in Gillingham and the neighbourhood.

The group which seceded under Mrs. Ann Rogers continued to flourish at their headquarters in Camden Road, London until the 1930s, and their weekly paper, the *Pioneer of Wisdom*, appeared regularly until December 1935. By that time the little group had passed under the leadership of Mr. George Bone, who functioned as trustee. In the December 1935 issue of the *Pioneer*

129

of Wisdom he announced the suspension of its publication, though at the same time he expressed the hope that publication would be resumed 'at a future date (D.V.)'. That hope has so far not been realized, and nothing more has been heard of the London group which Mrs. Ann Rogers led away from the Gillingham fold with so much élan.

The buildings which the 'New and Latter House of Israel' erected in its palmy days at Gillingham proved to be more durable than the sect itself. After the death of Mr. Naylar the builder of the tower, into whose possession it had come, the trustees of his estate put it up for auction at Tokenhouse Yard in London on September 6, 1897. The auctioneer stated breezily that he thought the tower could well be converted into a brewery or a lunatic asylum; and as a further inducement to prospective purchasers he mentioned that it contained not less than 620 tons of iron which ought to sell at £3 a ton, while the bricks and other material would pay for the cost of demolition. Moreover, he added, the seven acres of land surrounding the tower were ripe for development.

At this point a member of the audience asked whether there would be any difficulty in gaining possession. 'Not the slightest', said the auctioneer. The Jezreelites who were the existing tenants could be given three months' notice, and a purchaser could be guaranteed possession by Christmas. 'Suppose they won't go? They are very tenacious!' the inquirer replied, and added, 'You may have to carry on a young crusade to get them out!' The other persons attending the auction appeared to share these doubts, for bidding, which began at £3,000, stopped at £3,950, and as this was below the reserve price, the property was withdrawn.

It was later sold to three partners, who in 1905 made an agreement with a local builder that he should demolish the upper part of the tower. In February 1906, however, the builder went bankrupt, and thereafter the tower remained for many years a forlorn shell, with great jagged gaps in the upper brickwork where the builder's navvies had begun, but not completed, their work of demolition. In 1913 the tower was once more offered for sale at an auction in Tokenhouse Yard. The advertisement of the sale, in *The Times* of Saturday, February 15, 1913, said:

'ON CHATHAM HILL

'To manufacturers and others: In the heart of a densely-populated artisan district with ELECTRIC TRAMWAYS on both frontages. The valuable FREEHOLD PROPERTIES comprising the massive unfinished building known as "Jezreel's Temple", having an area of about 10,000 square feet on each floor, together with a range of buildings (230 feet long) originally erected as a college, but now used for club, restaurant and other purposes, and suitable for CONVERSION INTO SHOPS. Messrs. Brackett and Sons will sell the foregoing at the Mart, E.C., on Tuesday, March 4, at 2 p.m.'

The Times, commenting on the forthcoming sale in its issue of February 22, observed:

'The structural monstrosity of which an illustration appeared in *The Times* advertising columns last Saturday, known as "Jezreel's Temple" on Chatham Hill, Kent, is to come under the hammer of Messrs. Brackett and Son at Tokenhouse-yard on March 4.

It was founded many years ago by an ex-soldier, who claiming to be a second Elijah, collected his adherents at the spot and began building a "New and Latter House of Israel".

The career of the place has been chequered, but not stained by tragedies such as marked an earlier "religious" movement in the same county, when a young army officer was killed near Faversham in dispersing the followers of a notorious impostor.[1]

A great industrial centre has sprung up around the "Temple", and its future is probably commercial.'

At the auction on March 4 the property once more failed to find a purchaser, since the top bid, £3,900, was below the reserve price, and the lot was withdrawn. In October 1920 the property was offered to Gillingham Council for £2,500 but declined, and shortly afterwards the Gillingham Co-operative Society acquired it. The Society adapted the range of buildings fronting Canterbury Street as shops, and still retains these premises. The ruined

---

[1] A reference to the insurrection of a small band of Kentish farm-labourers led by Sir William Courtenay, *alias* John Nichols Tom, in 1838.

tower presented a greater problem; but finally its interior was made into hard tennis-courts, and a number of grass-courts were laid down in the grounds.

When the Second World War began all sorts of fantastic rumours began to circulate in the neighbourhood about the uses to which the famous tower was to be put. According to one report, however, the Government intended to demolish it regardless of expense because it would otherwise serve as a land-mark to guide the *Luftwaffe* to Chatham Dockyard and the many naval and military barracks and installations in the Medway Towns. Other know-alls, with some dim inkling of the coming of radar, acquired who knows how, whispered confidentially that the Government was going to put marvellous equipment at the top of the tower. This equipment would emit rays which would make aeroplane engines cut out, and spell disaster for the Germans. . . . In the event, however, neither of these predictions was fulfilled, and the tower emerged unscathed from the war. It might have been hoped, therefore, that having escaped the perils of bombing, the tower at least would be left undisturbed. But it was not to be. In December 1959 the Press reported that the Gillingham Co-operative Society had agreed to sell the tower and the adjacent land to a Gillingham industrialist who planned to demolish the tower completely, and use the site for a factory. It is only fair to state, however, that before the Society agreed to sell the tower to the industrialist it made an offer to the Gillingham Town Council. Feeling quite rightly that the structure ought to be preserved as a unique historical relic, the Society offered the tower to the Council at what was said to be a nominal price: but the Council declined the offer.

Future generations, if not this materialistic age, will surely condemn the refusal. Though, aesthetically-speaking, the tower was not an architectural masterpiece, it had, nevertheless, a certain grim, brooding majesty that was all its own. It was, also, in the truest sense of a much-abused word, unique. Gillingham had within its confines something of which there was no like any-where else in the world. It was a picturesque memorial of a strange myth which had brought the town frequently into the news for three-quarters of a century. The tower had been there so long, indeed, that it had become, seemingly, as integral a part of the Gillingham scene as the old parish church itself. The familiar bulk of the tower, silhouetted against the skyline on the top of Chatham Hill, visible for miles, was a sight that always induced a nostalgic pang in the returning traveller; and it seemed impossible that it should ever disappear.

Yet that day came. Demolition began in January 1960, and with modern equipment at work, the tough old tower began to break up at last. Wire hawsers were attached to the masonry, and when bulldozers, tractors and power-winches began to pull on these, Israel's proud sanctuary began to fall. The operations were viewed with disfavour by many local people who, although they were 'Gentiles', cherished the familiar old landmark; and one or two superstitious folk nodded their heads sagely and declared that no good would come of it all. The curse of Jezreel would infallibly descend on those who attempted to destroy his work.

Soon these prophets of woe nodded even more sagely, and their eyes gleamed triumphantly, and they said 'I told you so!' – for an unfortunate accident occurred on January 18. One of the lorry-drivers who were employed collecting the rubble resulting from the demolition was killed when about a hundred tons of masonry suddenly fell on him. During the inquest, at which a verdict of accidental death was returned, the coroner was told that the masonry in question had been carefully tested with powerful machinery the night before, to make sure that it was left in a safe condition. Giving evidence, the head of the demolition firm stated that the tower was 'like a fortress – very strong'. He and his men had stopped work the night before the accident feeling that the masonry of the tower was firm enough to stand fast for another hundred years.

The tragedy was proof positive, in the opinion of many local residents, that there was, as they said, a 'jinx' on the tower; but the demolition men did not share these apprehensions. The work of destruction went on steadily, and at last, on March 1, 1961, after fourteen months' heavy labour (the 'toughest of all tough jobs', as the demolition contractor described it), the sanctuary of Israel was no more. A small crowd of spectators watched the closing stages, and the occasion was honoured by the attendance of television operators. The tower had yielded, in all, nearly 6,000 tons of rubble, and this had been put to good use as foundations for the new bridge over the Medway near Rochester, and for other local building sites.

Local rumour, as active as ever whenever the tower was concerned, predicted that all kinds of sensational, and even gruesome discoveries would be made when the corner-stone was laid bare. As this final stage of the demolition work drew near, therefore, the crowd of spectators watched eagerly. The *Chatham and Rochester News*, on March 3, described the scene thus:

'Photographers clicked their shutters, television cameras whirred, and more than one hundred people gathered round in a tight little circle as workmen, armed with pneumatic drills, tried to free the foundation stone from the yellow brickwork surrounding it. The workmen chipped away with their chattering drills for more than half an hour, then one of them stepped back and said "It's no good, guv – it's too tough!"

Mr. H. A. Smith, the owner of the site, who was directing operations, brought a huge bulldozer into operation to turn the stone over.

Another half an hour went by, and the last bricks were coming away. Then one of the workmen shouted "There is something here!"

Then a copper and lead sealed cavity in the centre of the stone was uncovered, and the "secrets" were brought to light. . . . '

When the copper plate which covered the cavity in the foundation-stone was removed, however, no secrets were revealed, and the only articles found were those humdrum objects – a newspaper, coins, and a sheet of paper with an account of the foundation-stone-laying ceremony written on it – deposited by Mrs. Emma Cave on that gusty, rainy day in September 1885.[1] On September 26, 1885, reporting that memorable occasion, a

---

[1] The sheet of paper commemorating the ceremony and giving the names of those taking part is now preserved in Gillingham Library.

correspondent of the *Chatham and Rochester Observer* had presciently remarked:

'Even the Temple of Solomon had its day, and I am not so credulous as to suppose that the building of the "New and Latter House of Israel" will be more enduring. . . .'

Even he, however, sceptical as he was, could hardly have imagined that the great tower would not last a century, and that it would be pulled down efficiently and dispassionately, without protest from a generation which had become conditioned tamely to accept the gradual destruction of England's heritage of beautiful or strange buildings.

The fate of 'Woodlands', the rural retreat of Jezreel and Queen Esther, and, later, of Prince and Princess Michael, was as sad, and perhaps as regrettable as that of the tower. Like the latter building, 'Woodlands' could hardly be described as a beautiful building, especially after Louis Brennan added to it a lofty, depressing-looking water-tower. Nevertheless, there was something indefinably attractive about the house, perhaps because of the cosy way in which it nestled in the attractive grounds. A correspondent of the *Chatham and Rochester News* described the house in July 1888 as:

'peeping out from its picturesque surroundings. Clumps of white flowers' (he continued) 'relieve the green sward in front of the house, while it is flanked by a fine hedge of shrubs and wild roses. There is an air of comfort and quietness about "Woodlands" which cannot fail to impress the visitor.'

It is true that under Prince Michael's tenancy the house and grounds had deteriorated, but they were renovated after his followers left, and from 1928 until 1956 'Woodlands' was used as Gillingham Museum, housing a miscellaneous and rather motley collection of objects which had previously been on view under the old bandstand in Gillingham Park. In May 1956 however it was stated in the Press that Gillingham Council had decided to stop using 'Woodlands' as a museum because, so it was said, the building was unsuitable for the purpose and too remote. The museum was accordingly closed down on July 28, 1956. Suggestions were then made that the empty building might be used as a temporary school, or as a home for the chronic sick. These proposals were turned down, and the house remained empty. As the months went by the inevitable happened. Decay set in and in the autumn of 1958 the house was demolished as it had become unsafe. Proposals were afterwards made to erect a new building on the site to accommodate elderly people, but it remains to be seen whether these will be carried out.

Meanwhile (1962) the once lovely grounds resemble a wilderness. One cedar tree remains as a mute witness of the well-ordered past; but for the rest, garbage litters the drive, and little boys have made runways over the once-trim lawns and flower-beds with their bicycles. The scene is so shabby and dreary that a vivid effort of the imagination is required to realize that here, once, Jezreel the 'Messenger' dreamed his dreams, and saw his visions; that here too Esther queened it as the 'Mother of Israel', and Prince Michael ministered to the 'New Eve'.

Ichabod, Ichabod . . . the glory has, indeed, departed from Israel!

XIII

REFLECTIONS

A NY attempt to assess the historical, social or other significance of the Jezreelite cult must be based, to begin with,
on some estimate of the sect's membership. A considerable proportion of the members lived abroad, particularly in the
United States; but their exact number, and the number of those
living in Britain, cannot be ascertained because official returns of
membership were never made public. Statements made from time
to time by adherents, or former adherents, enable however a
rough estimate to be made.

When the sect was at the height of its prosperity, just before
Jezreel's death in 1885, there were said to be in all about 1,400
'regularly affiliated' members. By Queen Esther's death in 1888
the number of the faithful in all parts of the world had, according
to a statement made by an ex-member who claimed to know the
details, shrunk to about 250. Of these about thirty male members
lived in Gillingham and district, another thirty in Maidstone, and
about forty in London. About a hundred lived in other parts of
England, about twelve in Scotland, and the few who constituted
the remainder of the sect in the United States, Australia and New
Zealand. By 1894, after the secession of Mrs. Ann Rogers and her
followers, the 'remnant' left in Gillingham comprised no more
than about fifty persons, including women and children.

Thus even at the height of its prosperity the numbers of the
sect seem to have been remarkably small; and the question naturally arises, how, in such circumstances, could such a costly venture
as the sanctuary have been financed? The answer is to be found
in the very big contributions to funds made by several wealthy
individuals. Chief of these was Mrs. Emma Cave, who, the
Standard reported on July 2, 1888, had 'defrayed a considerable

portion of the outlay' on the tower. The *Chatham and Rochester Observer* on July 14, 1888, was more precise, and said that she had given 'thousands' to the cause, and there can be no doubt that she gave almost all that she had. When it is remembered that a number of other members, like Noah Drew, contributed sums of £1,000 or more to the 'treasury', that many smaller amounts were freely given, and that a steady stream of regular contributions, which rumour said amounted to a tithe of the income of members, also flowed in to Gillingham, the source of the funds which built the sanctuary and kept 'Woodlands' going is not far to seek.

It is more difficult, however, to explain how the sect came to establish such a hold on the members that many of them cheerfully beggared themselves to further the propagation of its doctrines. The purely religious aspect of the creed exerted, of course, a powerful attraction on many minds troubled and depressed by the Victorian emphasis on a physical hell to which sinners would be everlastingly consigned. Jezreel taught that hell was not eternal, and that all sinners would eventually be released from it. This doctrine alone was a comfort to many troubled souls; but when to it was added the promise that for 144,000 of the sealed there would be a complete redemption, denied to all others, the attraction became too great to be resisted; and many joined Jezreel's following because they hoped to become members of the immortal elect.

Fear, too, played a part in some cases. Because of the repeated warnings in the *Flying Roll* that the end of the final 'watch' was nigh, when Armageddon would be fought, and the sheep separated from the goats, some timid natures hastened to enrol in the 'New and Latter House of Israel' while there yet was time. The element of authoritarianism in the faith, exemplified by the special position which Jezreel claimed for himself, also made an appeal to many who yearned for guidance from an infallible leader, but were deterred, for one reason or another, from joining the Catholic Church.

Apart from religious factors, there can be no doubt that social considerations played a big part in drawing people into the fold.

Jezreel was wise enough not to impose too severe restrictions on his flock. Thus they were not denied the enjoyment of tobacco or alcohol, and were not made to wear a special uniform. Yet, on the other hand, he introduced sufficient distinguishing characteristics, chief of which was the long hair worn by the men, to enable the members to feel that they were, indeed, a closed community of the favoured few, a body set apart from the 'Gentiles'.

This feeling was encouraged by the establishment of the Jezreel trading concerns, by the foundation of Israel's International College, and, above all, by the private services of the sect. The thrill of being initiated into sacred mysteries undoubtedly had a powerful fascination for many people in an age when their emotional and imaginative faculties had far fewer outlets than they have today. The cinema, television, wireless and many other diversions help nowadays to keep boredom at bay; but the Victorians had none of these, and had very largely to provide their own distractions. Many of them sought release from the worries and monotony and drabness of everyday existence by joining some organized group or other, whether it was a working-men's club, a mechanics' institute, or a religious organization which offered more in the way of social activities than the large established denominations did. To people of this kind a small sect like the 'New and Latter House of Israel' was a social, as well as a religious necessity.

The fortunes of any organized group depend, however, to a large extent on the ability and energy of the leaders; and the Jezreelites proved no exception to this rule. Under Jezreel they thrived; under Esther they began to decay; under Edward Rogers they declined to insignificance. Jezreel, by any count, was a remarkable man. There was, to begin with, the mystery of his origin and his early years, which he sedulously propagated, and never resolved, even to Esther. There is no reason to believe that he had anything discreditable to hide. It simply paid him to remain the mysterious 'Messenger' or 'Trumpeter' or 'Stranger' who had arrived no one knew whence, and who might likewise one day depart, no one knew whither. The mystery appealed to the simple folk who had looked so long for the 'Trumpeter' or 'Messenger' who was to succeed John Wroe; and if newcomers to the sect ever asked, incautiously, about the leader's antecedents, they were told, in a hushed voice, that they must never, never inquire about such things. . . .

The mystery surrounding Jezreel's origin and early career will probably never be cleared up. It is far from certain that White was his real name, his place of birth he never disclosed; and even the date of his birth cannot be definitely stated to be 1840, though that, from the inscription on his coffin, is probably correct. Most unfortunately, perhaps, no photograph or painting of him was ever made, for, like John Wroe, he interpreted the second commandment literally. Only a general idea, therefore, can be gained of his physical appearance. He was a tall, imposing man nearly six feet in height, and well built. His long hair, when let down over his shoulders, and his luxuriant beard, combined to make a vivid impression on anybody who saw him for the first time; and the effect was enhanced by his piercing eyes, which were reputed to bore timid people 'through and through'.

He was a fluent and persuasive speaker, and always had a biblical quotation at hand to confute an opponent, or to clinch an argument of his own. It is easy to understand how, with his imposing presence and this ease of delivery, he was able to convince many credulous folk that he really was James, the inspired 'Messenger', whose writings and speeches were prompted by the 'Immortal Spirit'.

Yet he was not an original thinker. Most of the *Flying Roll* is a re-hash of Southcottian, particularly Wroeite, doctrine; and Jezreel's debt to the prophet of Ashton-under-Lyne was revealed in many other ways. Apart from the practice of letting the hair and beard grow long, which had been enjoined by Wroe on his followers, much of the ceremonial performed in the temple at Ashton was faithfully taken over by Jezreel and carried out during the private services of the 'New and Latter House of Israel'. Even Jezreel's conception of a great sanctuary had already been put into effect by Wroe.

Nevertheless Jezreel had some qualities peculiarly his own, and these contributed to his success. In the first place he was suave and diplomatic, and always managed to smooth over difficulties, were they with the Press or with recalcitrant followers, by glib evasions or by the exercise of his considerable charm. He was human, too; and could be very agreeable company. He enjoyed a joke, and was swift with repartee. It is significant that many of his followers still regarded him with affection even after they had decided to leave the fold. 'Ah! Mr. Jezreel! Now, he was a perfect gentleman!' was the sort of comment that several ex-members made on hearing of his death.

The 'Messenger' allied to his strong mystical personality a shrewd business sense and a commendable grasp of realities, together with a formidable capacity for sustained hard work. Not a little of the early success of the sect was due to the sound economic basis which Jezreel gave it by opening various shops and trading concerns. These soon acquired a well-deserved reputation for quality and fair-dealing, and undoubtedly raised the sect in the public esteem, as well as bringing in funds to the treasury.

Jezreel's business sense was shown by the way in which he put to work the large amounts of money which began to flow into the central fund. Sometimes he used it to acquire property to accommodate members of the sect; sometimes he bought land, which was cultivated to enable products to be supplied to the Jezreel shops at cost price; but a good deal of the money was invested in stocks and shares, and Jezreel paid frequent visits to his brokers in London in connection with his exchange transactions.

His capacity for work was enormous. Apart from acting as religious leader of the sect at various services, he closely supervised all the trading concerns, and also took a hand in the education of the pupils at Israel's International College. In addition he worked far into the night corresponding with members of the sect in all parts of the world; and as if all this was not enough for one man, he made frequent visits to the faithful in different parts of Britain, especially if they seemed wealthy enough to be worth cultivating. Because of this unremitting personal application to his work, he undoubtedly swelled the ranks of the 'New and Latter House of Israel', and swelled the coffers too. His exertions aggravated, however, a tendency to suffer from high blood pressure, and finally brought about his untimely death while at the height of his powers.

Malicious rumours were soon current that his death had been caused by excessive drinking; but there is absolutely no proof of this. There is likewise no proof that he was a sexual sadist, which is what the local Press left to be inferred when it printed lurid reports under such sensational headlines as 'Flogging Nude Girls'. It is significant that nobody ever came forward who had actually seen girls stripped and whipped at Jezreel's orders: always the accounts were by someone who had been told by someone else, who had it on good authority, etc., etc. The prosaic truth which lay concealed by all the rumours would seem to be simply that Jezreel, like many a Victorian paterfamilias, believed that to spare the rod was to spoil the child. Corporal punishment was therefore administered from time to time to youthful offenders; but, it would seem, always in a proper and normal way.

The local Press made tremendous play, naturally, with the rumour that there was a 'Black Hole' in 'Woodlands' in which Jezreel incarcerated members of the sect, including his own wife, who had annoyed him. Once again, it must be said that there is no proof. Nobody ever appeared who claimed to have *seen* people put in the 'Black Hole': the evidence was always second-hand, or third-hand, and not verifiable. On the other hand, it is quite possible that there was some truth in the stories that Jezreel had on several occasions turned Queen Esther out of 'Woodlands' because of quarrels. The lady was high-spirited and possessed a mind of her own; while Jezreel, like most Victorian husbands, claimed all the prerogatives as head of the family, and of course his spiritual precedence in addition. But even in this matter there is no proof; and there can be no doubt that even if there were occasional tiffs, the marriage between Jezreel and Esther was a very happy one.

Jezreel's unexpected, early death came as a great shock to his followers. Various theories were soon put forward to account for it, though none of them could really convince the doubters. One apologist declared that Jezreel himself had predicted that he would not live to see the completion of his work: thus the death of the prophet had been predestined. According to another theory put forward with diffidence, the 'good man' had proved not quite 'good enough', and had had imperfections of which he himself had been ignorant, leading to his early demise.

These uncertainties boded ill for the future of the sect, and had there not been on hand another strong personality it would probably have disintegrated there and then. The person who saved it for the time being was Jezreel's young wife, Queen Esther. In some respects she was a remarkable, in others a very ordinary woman: but by any standards her success in holding the 'New and Latter House of Israel' together after the catastrophic loss of the 'Messenger' was a great achievement.

She had been born of very humble parents, and had received hardly any formal education. Nevertheless, after she had fallen under the spell of the 'Messenger', at the age of fifteen, she seemed to develop anew. In place of the shy, somewhat backward girl there grew a vivacious young woman of strong views and great determination. The change was emphasized when, at the age of twenty-one, the young Clarissa Rogers left her family and friends to cross the Atlantic alone, and to sojourn among strangers in a far-off country.

The experience developed her still further; and when she returned to Gillingham she revealed the confidence of the successful missionary and the poise of a cultivated woman of affairs. It was little wonder therefore that Private James White on his return from India made Clarissa his bride as Mrs. Esther Jezreel. Had he searched the entire country, he would have found no woman more competent and qualified, and with enthusiasm equal to hers for the ambitious enterprises which he now had in mind.

Yet, while her husband was alive, Esther was content to remain in the background. When he died, however, her dynamism came at once into play. She routed Cumming and lesser contenders for the succession; and in a few weeks she had complete control of the sect, a control which she did not relinquish until death claimed her, too. It was a remarkable achievement, for she was only a young woman of twenty-five, whereas Cumming was old enough to be her grandfather and enjoyed great prestige among the faithful because of his age and experience. No doubt Esther's success was helped by the precedent established by Joanna Southcott: but the major factor was her own personality – a compound of ambition, ruthlessness and drive.

While her ambition to complete the sanctuary and to supervise the ingathering of the 144,000 was as great as Jezreel's, and while she could drive people as hard as he had done, she lacked her husband's capacity for sustained effort. She lacked, above all, his subtlety and tact, and her efforts to gain converts were, in comparison with his, somewhat crude. One person whom she approached told the *Chatham and Rochester Observer* (March 7, 1885):

'Mrs. Jezreel did everything she could to try to persuade me to read the *Flying Roll.* "Won't you come with us?" she inquired, "I *do* so wish you would join us! You are in utter darkness now, you know! I *do* so wish you would read this book!" Saying this she offered me a copy of the *Flying Roll.* On my declining it she repeated, "You are in utter darkness, now!" She tried at first to coax me into joining them by providing me with nice things to eat and drink; but after she found I refused, she changed towards me, and soon I was told not to come again.'

Esther was very tactless too in her mode of life. The 'Messenger' had lived frugally and unostentatiously: but Esther, once his restraining influence was gone, lived in style. At 'Woodlands' she had two bosom companions, Mrs. Emma Cave (in whose name the house was rented), and Mrs. Fanny Ball, whose functions can perhaps best be described as those of 'companion-housekeeper'. Both these ladies had been accustomed to luxury, and no doubt they partly influenced Esther in her new course. The new way of life at 'Woodlands' soon evoked much unfavourable, if covert comment from members of the sect who lived plain and sober lives on principle or, like Noah Drew, because they had to.

Esther's greatest mistakes, however, arose from her contemptuous disregard of other people's feelings. Her complete inability to take the human factor into account led her into such follies as the imposition of a month's fast. Worse still, it involved her in the discreditable affair of Noah Drew. If she had been less autocratic, less furious at having her will thwarted by Drew's refusal to move from his home in Gillingham High Street, she would have saved herself and the sect much unfavourable publicity and loss of goodwill. Had she been endowed with Jezreel's tact and perspicacity, she would have realized that at all costs the sect must be preserved from scandal, and that to give in to Drew would in the end prove the wisest course. As it was, the sect never entirely lived down the ill-repute which it gained locally through the treatment of Noah Drew.

Esther gradually became aware of growing opposition to her regime, but instead of trying to still it by living a simpler life and acting less imperiously, she adopted the methods employed by all dictators of setting spies to work. Soon within the 'New and Latter House of Israel' nobody could utter words of criticism without being sure that they would be carried to Queen Esther by one of the 'virgins' or other retailers of tittle-tattle on whom the duty fell of keeping the 'Mother of Israel' informed of all that was said and done.

As a result of Queen Esther's autocratic ways and refusal to listen to criticism, members began to leave the sect, or were 'cut-off'. The contributions flowing into the treasury began therefore to diminish; but Queen Esther pressed on fanatically, nevertheless, with her ambitious schemes, particularly with the building of the sanctuary. A month or two before her death the parlous state to which she had reduced the once flourishing finances was revealed when the builders ceased operations on the tower. Because of the rigorous control which she exercised the full extent of the disaster was not apparent till after her death; and by then dissensions within the sect prevented a financial recovery.

As soon as her firm control had gone the sect broke up. Edward Rogers did not claim to be more than 'steward' or 'overseer', but apart from that initial disadvantage, he quite lacked his daughter's strong personality and capacity to rule. He was a worthy man, but without the popular appeal which might have prevented disagreements from leading to secession. As it was, a major split occurred when Mrs. Ann Rogers led her group away to London, and that denoted the end of the 'New and Latter House of Israel' as a united, if declining body.

Prince Michael, it is true, appeared later on the scene to try to repair the rent garment of Israel; but his gaol sentence in the United States, apart from anything else, effectively ruined his chances of staging a revival of the Jezreelite fortunes. He was always regarded as a heretic by the members of the sect, no matter to which faction they belonged, and the details of his past, including his divorce, made his pretensions seem impious in the extreme to the members of the 'New and Latter House of Israel'.

They were deeply offended because they themselves were quiet, law-abiding folk, and apart from the vendetta waged against Noah Drew, they never did anything to draw upon themselves the dislike of their 'Gentile' fellow-citizens. On the contrary, they came to be regarded with something approaching affection, and this was rather remarkable, for they tended to keep very much to themselves, except for the everyday contacts which their businesses involved. Mostly, they belonged to what would be called the 'lower middle-class' and the 'working-class'; and it is noteworthy that Jezreel enrolled fewer well-educated and professional people amongst his followers than previous prophets, such as Brothers, Joanna Southcott, and John Wroe had done. Moreover, Jezreel made few converts among the 'Gentiles'. Most of his followers were won over from established Southcottian sects, like the 'Christian-Israelites' of John Wroe, so that they really only changed one version of the basic faith for another when they joined Jezreel.

Though the sect tended to attract, in general, ordinary working men and women of no great intellectual capacity or education, it also drew to itself some persons who were neurotic or of unbalanced mind. To such the strange mystical doctrines of the *Flying Roll*, couched in apocalyptic language, made an irresistible appeal. The confessions which were a feature of the private services also satisfied the strange but strong urges felt by the more emotional members of the sect. Here again, as in the desire to follow an infallible leader, a longing which could find no satisfaction in the protestant denominations, and which could otherwise be fulfilled only by joining the Catholic Church, drew many to the 'New and Latter House of Israel'.

One Jezreelite, at least, became so mentally unbalanced that he took his own life. The *Chatham and Rochester News*, on April 14, 1906, reported an inquest on Sidney Ashford, a member of the 'New and Latter House of Israel', whose body had been cut to pieces by a train at Woodlands Lane crossing, Gillingham. In Ashford's pockets a number of scraps of paper were found, bearing such inscriptions as:

'And Solomon, the wise man, had many wives, who drew his heart away from God to serve strange gods.'

During the inquest it was stated that Ashford, when a boy, had been an inmate for a time of the Kent County Lunatic Asylum at Barming, near Maidstone. At the end of the inquest a verdict of 'suicide during temporary insanity' was returned.

It must be stressed, however, that the vast majority of the Jezreelites were sane, ordinary men and women, who led pure, honest and hard-working lives. They found their daily strength and sustenance in the *Flying Roll*, for they believed that it had been divinely-inspired, and brought a message of supreme importance to mankind. After all the strange vicissitudes through which the sect has passed, a small number of adherents in Britain and the United States still have this belief, and they hope that one day the *Flying Roll* will be generally sought after.

It would be easy to adopt an attitude of scornful superiority, and dismiss these beliefs and hopes as foolish credulity. That, however, would be too harsh. Rather, it is surely a cause for wonder, and compassion too, that after so many cruel disappointments and blighted hopes, a few devoted souls still undauntedly believe in Jezreel and his *Flying Roll*.

A NOTE ON THE SOURCES

The two local papers, the *Chatham and Rochester News* and the *Chatham and Rochester Observer*, are the chief sources of information about the 'New and Latter House of Israel'. In addition the national and other papers and periodicals mentioned the sect from time to time. Among those which have been quoted the most important are:

Illustrated London News
Kent Messenger
Record
Standard
Strand Magazine
The Times

Other publications which were consulted include:

Balleine, G. R., *Past Finding out* (1956).
Dictionary of National Biography.
Jezreel, J. J., *Extracts from the Flying Roll* (1879–81).
Hazell's Annual Cyclopaedia (1887).
Knox, R. A., *Enthusiasm* (1950).
Leeds, C. S., *Chats about Gillingham* (1906).
Matthews, R., *English Messiahs* (1936).
Messenger of Wisdom and Israel's Guide (1887–1905).
Notes and Queries (1887).
Pioneer of Wisdom (1889–1935).
Quaife, M. M., *Lake Michigan* (1944).
Wilson, B. R., *Sects and Society* (1961).

INDEX

149

*Printed in Great Britain by
Cox and Wyman Limited
London, Reading and Fakenham*